What in the World Has Gotten into the Church?

Studies in the Book of Jude for Contemporary Christians

by
DAVID J. HESSELGRAVE
and
RONALD P. HESSELGRAVE

MOODY PRESS
CHICAGO

© 1981 by
THE MOODY BIBLE INSTITUTE
OF CHICAGO

All Scripture quotations, except those noted otherwise, are from the *New American Standard Bible,* © 1960, 1962, 1963, 1968, 1971, 1972, 1973, 1975, and 1977 by The Lockman Foundation, and are used by permission.

Verses designated NIV are from the Holy Bible: *New International Version.* Copyright © 1978 by the New York International Bible Society. Used by permission of Zondervan Bible Publishers.

The use of selected references from various versions of the Bible in this publication does not necessarily imply publisher endorsement of the versions in their entirety.

ISBN: 0-8024-9386-6

Printed in the United States of America

To Mr. and Mrs. Gust Swanson,
Rockford, Illinois,
Godly parents-in-law and grandparents,
Givers of gifts to the Church

Where "Church" is capitalized in this book, the authors are referring to the worldwide visible church; where it is not capitalized the reference is to the local congregation.

CONTENTS

FOREWORD

It isn't ordinary for a father and son to coauthor a book, but the Hesselgraves have never been ordinary. These fertile minds and warm spiritual hearts have produced a splendid, helpful book on Christians in a contemporary world. The surprise to the reader will be that the biblical text that forms the basis for this work is the oft-neglected book of Jude. The reader will find the exegesis constructive and the application, in the form of a set of questions at the end of each chapter, stimulating and informative.

As a faculty member of Trinity Evangelical Divinity School for nearly two decades, Dr. David Hesselgrave has dealt with the relation of Scripture to the contemporary world. As a distinguished professor of missions and world evangelism, his creativity and forethought has given birth to a Doctor of Missiology program and a School of World Mission and Evangelism that is world-renowned.

Ronald Hesselgrave spent most of his early life in Japan. He is a graduate of Trinity College and of Trinity Evangelical Divinity School with a Master of Divinity degree. He has a Master of Arts degree in history from the University of Illinois and is nearing completion of course work for his Ph.D. at Drew University. He has taught for two years at the Alaska Bible College.

This father and son combination has produced a biblically practical and applicable treatment of some of the most interesting and neglected verses in the New Testament. Today's need for a continued relating of Scripture to life's problems is most apparent. The Hesselgraves add an important dimension to our thinking about Christian living in our contemporary world through this solid and informative book *What in the World Has Gotten into the Church?* The quality of this book speaks to the caliber of their scholarship and practical Christian lives.

KENNETH M. MEYER
President, Trinity Evangelical Divinity School
Deerfield, Illinois

7

PREFACE

Sons are seldom carbon copies of their fathers. And that is as it should be. Sons must do their own thinking and live their own lives. Fathers have sufficient cause for gratitude to God if their sons share their basic faith, values, and commitment. And sons have equal cause for gratitude if in the crucibles of study and experience they discover their father's faith to be a firm foundation, fit for life and service.

As father and son we share a common commitment to Christ, His Word, and His Church. Our highest aspirations in the writing of this book will be served if this book brings glory to Christ, attention to the Scriptures, and purity and strength to His Church.

We do not in every case agree on matters of interpretation, however. Where we do not agree we have simply commended the alternatives to the further consideration of the reader. After all, Jude spoke to a variety of issues that could not be fully explored in his divinely inspired and abbreviated letter. Nor can they be comprehensively considered in our brief and feeble effort to expand on it. Let believing readers exercise their priesthood by searching the Scriptures on these matters and becoming persuaded in their own minds.

Our thanks to Dr. Douglas Moo of the New Testament faculty at Trinity Evangelical Divinity School, who read the manuscript and made some valuable suggestions. Also to parents, grandparents, teachers, and colleagues who have contributed so much to our understanding of the Word and our love for the Church. Of course, errors and weaknesses accrue to our own account.

> *"The church must be in the world;*
> *the world must not be in the church."*
>
> The Lausanne Covenant,
> paragraph 12

Part One

PRELIMINARIES

1

PANDORA'S BOX AND THE TWENTIETH-CENTURY CHURCH

INTRODUCTION

Here is the church,
Here is the steeple;
Open it up,
And see all the people!

People indeed. And not only *"all* the people," but all *kinds* of people. Educated people and unlearned people; saintly people and unsavory people; very gifted people and very ordinary people—and multitudes in between those extremes. James Pike, Billy Graham, John A. T. Robinson, Bob Jones, Sr., Paul Tillich, Jim Jones, David O. Berg, Fulton J. Sheen—and a host of others, known and unknown, claim to be part of the Church. What a variety of people are to be found in the Church!

And what a confusing collection of *teachings* are to be found in the Church. Catholic and Protestant theologies, liberal and conservative theologies, Calvinistic and Arminian theologies, traditional and contextualized theologies; God-is-dead theology, liberation theology, black theology, waterbuffalo theology, the theology of the pain of God, and the theology of hope—to name just a few.

And what about the bewildering succession of *activities* to be found in the churches? Of course, there are those multitudinous accomplishments that merit the praise of everyone. But what about

11

the burning of draft cards, the provision of mission money for marauding guerrillas, the ordination of homosexuals, worship with nude dancers, Christ portrayed as a superstar and a clown, and . . . The list seems endless.

What's Gotten into the Church?

Why is it that the Church has become the arena of such confusion? What in the world has gotten into it?

The world!

So we should not be surprised. Look at the world. Every part of the world touched by man has also been polluted by man.

He has occupied the lithosphere (the solid part of the earth), and he has polluted it by exposing it to the forces of erosion, covering it with asphalt and concrete, and defacing it with the scars of his machines.

He has invaded the hydrosphere (the waters of the earth) and has polluted it with chemicals and garbage until sea life is threatened.

He has projected himself into the atmosphere (the gaseous envelope around the earth) and has polluted it with the fumes of his factories and engines and with the debris of his space technology.

He has bombarded the "ideosphere" (the sphere of ideas and values) and has polluted it with the results of his unaided rationality and unbridled animality until great numbers of his kind live without meaning or morals.

The fact that there is much in the Church that stands out in stark contrast to that which we see in other areas of human life is due to the gracious activity of God in the individual lives and corporate life of His people. Much (no, most) of that which is good in the world is to be found in the Church—honest people, wholesome teaching, and kindly deeds. To the degree that the Church is populated by true believers who have been transformed by God's grace and are being conformed to Christ's image, it contains the salt and light of the world.

That is what we would expect. After all, the Word of God is heard there, so there is *truth* in the Church; the Holy Spirit resides in God's people, so there is *power* in the Church; and Christ is building it, so there is *hope* in the Church. It may come as a surprise to some, but the Church is growing—especially in Africa, Latin America, and parts of Asia.

Nevertheless, it is true that in this massive and multiform entity called the Church there are persons, teachings, and goings-on that one would not expect to find in a divinely ordained institution. Ordinary observers must be repeatedly surprised at the oddities that emerge from the doors of the churches. And careful investigators must be equally surprised at the absurdities discoverable behind them.

Why?

Because the "world" has gotten into the Church. Like the *torii*, or gate, which is designed to shut out evil spirits but which stands impotent before every Shinto shrine, just so the discernment and discipline divinely designed to garrison many churches have been lowered to the point where the world can enter without a challenge.

HOPE IN THE CHURCH

One hesitates to make odious comparisons, but the Church seems rather like a certain Pandora's box. You may remember that, according to Greek mythology, Prometheus stole some fire from heaven. In retaliation, Zeus sent a woman named Pandora to earth. She was given a box containing all sorts of human ills, some of which emerged each time the box was opened. Hope was also in the box— but there it remained!

Unlike Pandora's box, the Church is in no sense mythical. It is very real. And so are the *ills* that all too frequently emerge from it. But so also is the *hope* that is in the Church. The challenge that confronts those of us who are Christians is to make that hope more visible and believable!

Almost two thousand years ago Jude wrote about the Church. He recognized that the Church of his day was a "mixed box," too. He explained that men who had no business being in the Church— heretics and apostates—had "crept in" (*pareisdunō*, v. 4) and were parading about. He described them and their teachings so they could be recognized. He depicted their end so their judgment could be avoided. He defended true faith and practice so that hope would prevail. And he did all of this under the inspiration of the Spirit of God—the Spirit of truth and holiness.

Today as never before, we Christians need to understand the world in which we live—its spirit, its suffering, its ills, its despair. We also need to understand the Church—its purpose, its power, its predicament, its potential. It is dangerous not to know what the world has determined to be in its rebellion against God. And it is equally dangerous not to know what the Church is destined to be in the plan of God. *We need to study both the world and the Church. But most of all we need to study the Word of God. Only in its light can we maintain a proper perspective as our earth spins madly into its tumultuous tomorrows with our churches still clinging to its surface.*

Few portions of the divine Word are more relevant to our troubled times than is the book of Jude. To that book we now turn.

QUESTIONS FOR REFLECTION AND DISCUSSION

1. Think of the world and the Church. Both are made up of people who have ideas, purposes, and life-styles. What should be the major difference between the world and the Church?
2. Before we proceed with our study of Jude's letter, think of your church and take a preliminary inventory. What are its strengths? What are its weaknesses (assuming that there are some)? Do the weaknesses parallel or mirror ideas, attitudes, or behavioral patterns that can be termed "worldly?"

2

JUDE'S EPISTLE AND THE FIRST-CENTURY CONTEXT

Jude, a bond-servant of Jesus Christ, and brother of James, to those who are the called, beloved in God the Father, and kept for Jesus Christ: May mercy and peace and love be multiplied to you. Beloved . . .

JUDE 1-3

The author	Jude (Judas), the brother of James and half-brother of Jesus (?)
The date	Likely between A.D. 75-85
The place	Palestine
The addressees	Christians in the churches of Syria or Asia Minor
The purpose	To instruct and warn believers concerning worldly people who were in their churches

INTRODUCTION

God has an important message for us in the epistle of Jude. Otherwise it would not be in His holy Word, the Bible. But, as every teacher of communication and interpretation will emphasize in his introductory lecture, if we want to get the message intended by God and Jude we must ask questions like: Who was writing to whom? For what reason? and, Under what circumstances? The inspired

15

authors of Scripture—including Jude—do not always supply clear answers to all of those questions. Nor does external evidence always supply the answers. We may safely assume, however, that God has seen to it that we have as much information as is necessary to understand His intended message in any given book of the Bible. On the basis of that assumption we will proceed to explore those questions with reference to the epistle before us.

WILL THE AUTHOR PLEASE STAND?

We often speak of Jude as though we know him well enough to pick him out of any crowd. Not so. In fact, we must make some inquiries if we are to establish his identity.

You can call the writer of this epistle Judah (Hebrew), Judas (Greek), or Jude (English). It is the same name. The name was a common one in ancient Palestine—something like the name *Robert* today. There must have been thousands of Judes in first-century Palestine. Five of them appear in the New Testament:

1. Judas of Damascus (Acts 9:11)
2. Judas called Barsabbas (Acts 15:22)
3. Judas Iscariot (Mark 3:19)
4. Judas the apostle, also called Thaddaeus (Matthew 10:3; Mark 3:18), and "the son [or brother] of James" (Luke 6:16; Acts 1:13)
5. Judas, our Lord's brother (Matthew 13:55; Mark 6:3)

It is reasonable to assume that the author of the letter before us was one of those five. But which one? Certainly not Judas Iscariot. Likely not Judas of Damascus or Judas called Barsabbas. If this line of reasoning is valid, out of a cast of thousands, we are down to two. The author is likely either Judas the apostle or Judas our Lord's brother.

But wait a minute. There is still another possibility. It could be that Judas the apostle and Judas the brother of our Lord were one and the same person. There is a good possibility that Jude was the son of Mary, mother of Jesus, and therefore a half-brother of our Lord and brother of James, the more famous head of the Jerusalem church (v. 1).[1]

We will conjecture, then, that the author of the letter before us is Jude the apostle and brother of our Lord. But we cannot be dogmatic. Neither the internal nor the external evidence is at all conclusive.

". . . PALESTINE, THE YEAR OF OUR LORD . . ."

Is it possible to ascertain the author's address and the date of this letter? Yes and no. Certainly we cannot pinpoint the time and place. But certain generalizations are possible.

If Jude himself wrote the letter (and there is no reason to doubt that), it must have been written in the apostolic age and probably in neither the earlier nor later parts of that age. By the time Jude's epistle was written, the apostolic faith was crystalized (v. 3); the words of the apostles could be recalled (v. 17); and some of their warnings had already been fulfilled (v. 18). Also, it is unlikely that the condition of the church he described could have developed in the earliest days of the Church. All of that suggests a somewhat later date—perhaps beween A.D. 75 and 85.

As to the place of writing, we can only say that it was probably written in Palestine. After all, there is nothing to indicate that Jude lived anywhere else. And though an argument from silence has limited evidential value, it is reinforced by the references and tone of the letter, which appear to be Palestinian.

"DEAR FELLOW-CHRISTIANS"

Jude's letter can be read quite leisurely in three or four minutes. In a day when the "really good" sermon is about twenty minutes in length—and certainly no longer than thirty minutes—this letter should command a dedicated readership. But such is not the case. As a matter of fact, Jude's bantam book receives scant attention in the Church and almost none outside of it. Why?

In an earlier day, Jude's epistle was neglected by some because it contains references to certain apocryphal writings. From the fourth century on, however, its canonical authority has been unchallenged in the Western Church. Perhaps it is neglected today because of our notion that in addition to being brief, the good sermon

(or Bible study or religious book) should be affirmative and positive. Jude's letter is positive, of course, but not until the very end.
From the outset, it prophesies and portrays spiritual defections and
disasters. That approach does not "grab us" as contemporary
Christians. Perhaps we secretly hope that if we ignore the portrayal
and prophecy they will not come true—at least not wholly true.

Jude is not a spiritual sadist. He wants to be positive in his approach. He wants simply to dwell on the great things God has done
for His people and write about our great salvation (v. 3). But he
is a realist. So he writes of a mental and moral malignancy that
threatens the churches. He does not spell out all the specifics concerning the threat, but obviously he believes that the situation is
serious and needs to be dealt with directly and swiftly.

An important insight is to be gained here. Only those who earnestly desire to major on God's "so great salvation" are justified in
dwelling upon the erroneous teachings, attitudes, and actions that
abrogate it. If a teacher becomes wholly preoccupied with error in
the Church, there is a strong likelihood that his spirit will become
sour, critical, and abrasive. In order to remain winsome and balanced, one's spirit must delight in the salvation that God offers to
His people. It is the teacher who wants to major on salvation who
is best qualified to warn against error because, inevitably, he will do
it with compassion in his heart, a tear in his eye, and compulsion in
his voice.

The designation "general epistle" commonly given to Jude's book
is really misleading because it is clear that Jude has in mind a
specific situation involving a specific church or group of churches.
Which church or churches is a matter of some conjecture. But much
can be said for the view that they were located in Syria or Asia
Minor. Strong support for that comes from the many obvious paral-
lels between Jude and 2 Peter. From the introduction to the latter
book we know that that area was the destination of Peter's epistle.
And it seems likely that Peter and Jude are combating the same
opponents.[2]

Even though Jude does not identify his opponents by name or
school, he does give us a fairly complete picture of their charac-

teristics and practices. In their theology they were antinomian (vv. 4, 12), displaying an arrogant disrespect for divine authority (vv. 4, 8). They gained followers and generally made their presence felt in the Church through deception, flashy rhetoric, and strong charismatic appeal (vv. 4, 12, 16). They had few scruples. For them, religion was a business to be engaged in for what one could get out of it (vv. 12, 16). They practiced loose living sexually and were proud of it (vv. 8, 12). They were rabble-rousers and schismatics (v. 16).

All of that suggests striking similarities to certain early heretics known as Gnostics, whose forerunners were present in the churches as early as the second half of the first century. Gnosticism has been defined as "a system of thought which taught the cosmic redemption of the spirit through knowledge."[3] Gnostics believed that some people were so intellectually and spiritually superior that they could become as good as (or better than) Jesus and attain direct union with God.[4] One who is truly "spiritual," they reasoned, has received divine grace and is not capable of sin. Consequently, such a person is free from the moral restraints that bind ordinary people, who are still trapped in the material world. Gnostics were "dead wrong," but they (and other heretics) endangered the early Church. And Jude knew it. That is why he wrote this letter.

CONCLUSION

As contemporary Christians we may close our eyes to present danger in the Church and wish that it were not present, that heretics such as Jude describes were absent, that the malignancy has been cured, and that we can confine our attention to the great salvation concerning which Jude wants to write but cannot. But when we open our eyes and view the Church we know it is not so. Times and people change. The modern counterparts to Jude's protagonists may alter their style to fit contemporary patterns. But they are present inside and outside the Church, and their teachings prosper. Like it or not, Jude's theme is as relevant as the warning label on a bottle of poison.

NOTES

1. "Brothers of the Lord" (as in 1 Corinthians 9:5) can mean "cousins," however. James and Jude, then, may have been sons of Mary and Cleopas (the same as Alphaeus) and apostles, as Jerome held.
2. George L. Lawler, *Translation and Exposition of the Epistle of Jude* (Nutley, N.J.: Presbyterian and Reformed Pub., 1972), p. 9.
3. Jaroslav Pelikan, *The Christian Tradition: A History of the Development of Doctrine: The Emergence of Catholic Tradition*, 3 vols. (Chicago: U. of Chicago Press, 1971), 1:82.
4. William Barclay, *The Letters of John and Jude* (Philadelphia: Westminster, 1960), pp. 165-66.

QUESTIONS FOR REFLECTION AND DISCUSSION

1. How is it possible to have confidence that the book of Jude is part of the fully authoritative Word of God when we cannot identify the author and the time and place of writing with complete confidence?

2. The churches have numerous critics who can see no good in the Church. It has some defenders who seem unable to see any errors or weaknesses in it. Why is it difficult to be balanced and objective in evaluating the Church and local churches?

3

HONEST TO GOD—AND TO THE WORLD AND THE CHURCH

Beloved, while I was making every effort to write you about our common salvation, I felt the necessity to write to you appealing that you contend earnestly for the faith which was once for all delivered to the saints. For certain persons have crept in unnoticed, those who were long beforehand marked out for this condemnation, ungodly persons who turn the grace of our God into licentiousness and deny our only Master and Lord, Jesus Christ.

JUDE 3-4

Definition	Heresy: an opinion or teaching that is not in accord with commonly received doctrine and that tends toward division
	Apostasy: the abandonment of essentials of the faith once professed
Description	*Asebeia:* irreverence, ungodliness
	Aselgeia: sensuality, immorality
	Anomia: lawlessness, denial of lordship
Disposition	Judgment beginning in the Church
	Judgment engulfing the world

INTRODUCTION

To contend for truth requires that one be truthful. Of course, one must also be committed to God and concerned for mankind. But commitment and concern must be accompanied by honesty. Jude understands that. He wastes no time letting his readers know exactly what those false teachers "look like." If Christians have identifying marks (and they do according to John 13:35), so do heretics and apostates. If *orthodoxy* is demonstrated by *orthopraxy* (and it is according to James 1:27), so is *heterodoxy* characterized by *heteropraxy*.

HERESY AND APOSTASY—EITHER/OR OR BOTH/AND?

We have used the words "heresy" and "apostasy." Before going further we should define those words to see whether they fit the false teachers Jude describes.

The word *heresy* is derived from the Greek verb *hairein*, which means "to take" or "to choose." As a noun it occurs only once in the New Testament (Titus 3:10). As an adjective it occurs twice (1 Corinthians 11:19; Galatians 5:20). It refers to teachings and actions that are not in accord with commonly received doctrine and therefore tend toward division and schism. As Charles Ryrie points out, heresy belongs to those works of the flesh that are often characteristic of carnal Christians (Galatians 5:20).[1]

The word *apostasy* is derived from the Greek prefix *apo* and the verb *stēnai*. Together they mean "to stand away from" or "off from." The verb occurs some fourteen times in the New Testament, and in almost every case it refers to an abandonment of essentials of faith once professed.[2]

Strictly speaking, therefore, heresy and apostasy should be carefully distinguished. The heretic may well be a believer who needs counsel and discipline, repentance and restoration, instruction and growth. The apostate has willfully departed from the faith and stands in opposition to the body of Christian truth.[3]

How, then, should we categorize the false teachers and false practitioners referred to by Jude? It is very possible that Jude con-

sidered the presence of those false teachers to be a part of the fulfillment of Paul's prediction that in the latter times some would
"abandon the faith" (Jude 17; 1 Timothy 4:1). Moreover, Jude
says that those people do not have the Spirit (Jude 19), and we
know that those who do not have the Spirit of Christ do not belong
to Him (Romans 8:9). Jude may not have been making a fine
distinction between those categories, but the evidence suggests that
he was primarily concerned with apostates—and, perhaps, heretics
of an extreme type—and their presence in, and influence upon, the
churches.

THE MARKS OF APOSTASY

In warning his readers that false teachers have crept into their
fellowship, Jude immediately points out three characteristics that
mark them (v. 4). He does not mince words. First, they are god-
less (*asebeia*). Second, they change God's grace into a license for
immorality (*aselgeia*). Third, they are guilty of lawlessness
(*anomia*), denying our Sovereign and Lord, Jesus Christ. The first
two of the words are explicit in the text; the third one is implicit.
Without being technical, those Greek words can be thought of as
referring to the sin of the spirit (the "God-conscious" part of man),
the sin of the body (the "world-conscious" part of man), and the
sin of the soul (the "self-conscious" part of man).

What a damning indictment! But Jude has only *started* by noting
those characteristics; he does not *stop* with them. Throughout the
body of his letter he elaborates, illustrates, and otherwise portrays
the marks of apostasy. Note the following references:

EXPLANATIONS AND DESCRIPTIONS

1. They are dreamers who pollute their own bodies (v. 8).
2. They reject authority (v. 8).
3. They slander celestial beings (v. 8).
4. They speak abusively against whatever they do not understand
   (v. 10).
5. They are being destroyed by things that they instinctively understand (v. 10).

6. They are the subjects of Enoch's prophecy (v. 14).
7. They commit ungodly acts in an ungodly way (v. 15).
8. They are grumblers and faultfinders (v. 16).
9. They follow their own desires (v. 16).
10. They boast about themselves (v. 16).
11. They flatter others for their own advantage (v. 16).
12. They are the subjects of apostolic prophecy (v. 17).
13. They are scoffers, or mockers (v. 18).
14. They follow their ungodly desires (v. 18).
15. They cause divisions among believers (v. 19).
16. They follow natural instincts (v. 19).

PRECURSORS AND EXAMPLES

1. The unbelieving people of the Exodus (v. 5)
2. The fallen angels (v. 6)
3. Sodom, Gomorrah, and surrounding towns (v. 7)
4. The archangel Michael's refusal to slanderously accuse the devil (v. 9)
5. Cain's way (v. 11)
6. Balaam's error (v. 11)
7. Korah's rebellion (v. 11)

METAPHORS AND ANALOGIES

1. Hidden reefs at love feasts (v. 12)
2. Shepherds who starve the flock (v. 12)
3. Windblown, rainless clouds (v. 12)
4. Fruitless, rootless autumn trees (v. 12)
5. Wild, foaming waves of the sea (v. 13)
6. Wandering stars (v. 13)

TIME FOR JUDGMENT—BEGINNING AT THE HOUSE OF GOD

What an extensive catalogue of evil for such a short letter! It would appear that Jude is so angered by the intrusion of these heretics and apostates into the assemblies of the faithful that he simply vents his anger by recording whatever evil epithets come to his mind. We should not jump to that conclusion, however. That

Jude feels righteous indignation is both unnecessary and impossible to deny.

But his words do not represent a gushing forth of mindless and unmeasured anger. Not at all. Rather, he has thought things through. Under Holy Spirit guidance, he reinforces precisely those charges made in his basic indictment in verse 4. One need not stretch or bend Jude's subsequent statements to make them fit that basic pattern. In them Jude simply reiterates, amplifies, and otherwise describes the irreverence, immorality, and lawlessness that characterize many heretics in the first century *and* in the twentieth.

But, of course, merely saying that Jude's description fits today's situation does not make it true. So let us call forth witnesses. Listen to people from the world and from the churches. Watch the media. Read what is being written. Hear what people are saying. Examine the evidence. What is happening inside and outside the Church? What are people doing? What does the record say?

Unlike Jude, however, we do not possess apostolic authority and divine inspiration. Are we then qualified to pass judgment on heretics and apostates today?

In one sense, no. Saints and sinners, vessels of honor and vessels of dishonor, teachers who are holy and apostolic and teachers who are heretical and apostate—both kinds of people will be present inside and outside the Church until the end of the age. Vengeance belongs to God. He will repay. Our main task is not to engage in witch-hunts in a desperate attempt to rid the world and the churches of all that is demonic and degrading. As someone has said, "There is so much bad in the best of us, and so much good in the worst of us that it hardly behooves any of us to talk about the rest of us!"

In another sense, yes. Judgment must begin at the house of God (1 Peter 4:17). False teachers are to be pointed out and opposed: "Watch out for those who cause divisions and put obstacles in your way that are contrary to the teaching you have learned" (Romans 16:17, NIV)* The teacher who "runs ahead and does not continue in the teaching of Christ" is not to be received or even greeted (2 John 9-10, NIV). And those who call themselves brothers while

*New International Version.

living in sin are to be dealt with differently than sinners in the world:

> I have written you in my letter not to associate with sexually im-
> moral people—not at all meaning the people of this world who are
> immoral, or the greedy and swindlers, or idolaters. In that case
> you would have to leave this world. But now I am writing you
> that you must not associate with anyone who calls himself a
> brother but is sexually immoral or greedy, an idolater or a slan-
> derer, a drunkard or a swindler. With such a man do not even
> eat.
>
> What business is it of mine to judge those outside the church?
> Are you not to judge those inside? God will judge those outside.
> "Expel the wicked man from among you." [1 Corinthians 5:9-13,
> NIV]

Accordingly, the whole thrust of Jude's letter makes clear that
false teachers are to be identified, that their teachings are to be rejected, that their example is to be eschewed, and that their end is to
be deplored.

CONCLUSION

Woe to the Christian who is concerned for personal salvation only and not for the purity of the Church and the perpetuation
of the faith. In the beginning he simply jades the testimony of the
local Body of Christ. In the end he seriously jeopardizes the Christian mission to the whole world.

NOTES

1. Charles Ryrie, "Apostasy in the Church," *Bibliotheca Sacra,* January 1964, p. 47.
2. Ibid., p. 45.
3. Ibid., p. 47.

QUESTIONS FOR REFLECTION AND DISCUSSION

1. Read 2 Timothy 3:1-9 and 4:3-4. In the light of Jude's warning
    in verses 3 and 4, what do those verses tell us about the forms in
    which unbelief can be present in the churches without being
    fully detected? How does Paul's description of false teachers
    compare with the characteristics given by Jude?

2. What is the significance of the various metaphors and analogies Jude uses to characterize apostasy? What is their particular value?
3. How would you respond to the argument that judgment is inconsistent with belief in a God of love?
4. Given the biblical principle that judgment must begin at the house of God, what kind of judgment is wrong as far as believers are concerned (Romans 2:1-3; 14:1-12; 1 Corinthians 4:1-5; James 4:11-12)? What kind of judgment is right (Matthew 7:15-23; 24:24; 1 Timothy 6:3-5; 2 John 9-10)?

4

IRREVERENCE—THE SIN OF THE SPIRIT

For certain persons have crept in unnoticed, those who were long beforehand marked out for this condemnation, ungodly persons. . . .

JUDE 4

	Irreverence
Designation	*Asebeia*—ungodliness, impiety, irreverence (v. 4)
Explanations and descriptions	1. "Revile angelic majesties" (v. 8) 2. "Revile [speak abusively]" (v. 10) 3. "Ungodly deeds which they have done" (v. 15) 4. "Grumblers, finding fault" (v. 16) 5. "Mockers" (v. 18)
Metaphors and analogies	"Hidden reefs in your love feasts" (v. 12)
Precursors and examples	1. The people of the Exodus (v. 5) 2. Michael the archangel (v. 9) 3. The way of Cain (v. 11)

INTRODUCTION

Christians and unbelievers, Christian teachings and un-Christian teachings, and Christian practices and un-Christian practices—

those are usually clearly distinguishable. The former are found in the Church, and the latter are found in the world.

Jude monitors the Church television screen while the surveillance camera zeros in on some suspicious characters and their activity. Sure enough, upon close examination they prove to be worldlings. Worldly people, propositions, and practices have gotten into the Church without being noticed. So Jude points them out for all to see. He produces proofs of their worldliness. As long as they are in the Church they will be marked men, ideas, and activities.

What are the proofs?

As we noted in the last chapter, the first one is a spirit of irreverence—a spirit totally out of place anywhere and especially in the churches. But there it is as big as life occupying both pew and pulpit. Ironic, isn't it? Even "Reverends" can be irreverent!

JUDE ON IRREVERENCE

Jude's word for "ungodly" (v. 4) is *asebeia*. A reading of this short letter in the original language gives the impression that *asebeia* is one of his favorite words. In various forms it occurs six times in this short letter. But, of course, the impression is incorrect. Jude does not use the word because he is fascinated by it. He uses it because it fits the facts.

EXPLANATIONS AND DESCRIPTIONS

What, exactly, is *asebeia?* It is ungodliness and impiety. It is irreverence. Look at the text, and it will become more apparent what Jude has in mind. Words and phrases that seem parallel include the following:

1. They "revile angelic majesties" (v. 8). A literal rendering would be "blaspheme angelic glories." Using contemptuous speech they intentionally come short of giving the glory due. At one level, to be irrevent means "to make a joke of" (J. B. Phillips translates it, "[They] make a jest of the heavenly glories"). At another level, to be irreverent means to reproach or revile.

2. They "revile the things . . . they do not understand" (v. 10).

3. They "commit irreverent acts in an irreverent way" (v. 15, authors' trans.).

4. They are "grumblers, finding fault" (v. 16). And this they are before God!

5. They are "mockers" (v. 18). The word here is *empaizō,* which means "to play." Instead of testifying to the truth, these teachers toy with the truth.

METAPHORS AND ANALOGIES

Of the various related metaphors and analogies used by Jude, one is most apt: "These men are . . . hidden reefs in your love feasts when they feast with you without fear" (v. 12). What gathering could be more peaceful and hopeful than a group of Christians at the table of the Lord? But even there appearances can be deceiving. When people who do not fear God are at that table—especially at *that* table—danger is present. Paul's word to the Corinthians applies:

> In the following directives I have no praise for you, for your meet-ings do more harm than good. In the first place, I hear that when you come together as a church, there are divisions among you, and to some extent I believe it. No doubt there have to be differ-ences among you to show which of you have God's approval. When you come together, it is not the Lord's Supper you eat, for as you eat, each of you goes ahead without waiting for anybody else. One remains hungry, another gets drunk. Don't you have homes to eat and drink in? Or do you despise the church of God and humiliate those who have nothing? What shall I say to you? Shall I praise you for this? Certainly not! [1 Corinthians 11:17-22, NIV]

PRECURSORS AND EXAMPLES

Finally, Jude gives some examples of that kind of behavior from the Old Testament:

1. *The people of the Exodus* (v. 5). In calling attention to the people who were brought out of Egypt, Jude simply says that they "did not believe" (v. 5). The most obvious reference is to Numbers

14:27-37 where we find that, with the exceptions of Caleb and Joshua, the people were consigned to death in the wilderness because they refused to believe that the God who promised was able to "deliver the goods" (the promised land). Then they murmured against God (cf. Jude 16). Indeed, when Paul catalogs the failings of Israel in his first letter to the Corinthians he concludes by calling attention to their complaining (1 Corinthians 10:10).

Now grumbling and murmuring are never praiseworthy. But the children of Israel were guilty of complaining "in the hearing of the LORD" (Numbers 11:1-9). God hears all complaints, but those particular complaints were lodged in the very ears of Jehovah. The people decried the manna that God miraculously rained from heaven. They longed for the fish, cucumbers, melons, leeks, onions, and garlic that they had enjoyed in Egypt. They seemingly cared little that the fare of Egypt fueled insufferable labors and degradation, whereas manna was sent to nourish their journey to the promised land. In any case, how can it be that the dust of humanity dare speak out against the Deity of heaven? No wonder Jehovah judged some by fire.

2. *Michael the archangel as an example of reverent fear* (v. 9). It is possible to overestimate the greatness of angels. Evidently some people in the early churches went so far as to worship them (Colossians 2:18). But far from worshiping angels, the people indicated by Jude "pooh-poohed" them. They literally slandered celestial beings (v. 8). Peter says the same thing (2 Peter 2:10). We might think that is a small matter. But we will not think so if we recognize angels as the exalted messengers of the God of the universe. As a matter of fact, the attitude of the archangel Michael testifies against such irreverence even in the case of the fallen angel Satan (v. 9).

Michael is mentioned in Daniel 10:13, 21; 12:1; and Revelation 12:7. But the record of Michael's disputing with the devil over the body of Moses is found in the apocryphal book *The Assumption of Moses*. Jude's use of the incident does not confer historical validity on all that is to be found in that book, but it does constitute a testimony to the factualness of that particular incident.

Jude's point is clear. Michael exalted God and recognized that judgment belongs to Him alone. Archangel though he was and is, he himself simply did not dare to pronounce a judgment against even the devil. In the light of that, the slightest disregard of the Divine Person—or even against members of His heavenly retinue—becomes unthinkable.

3. *The way of Cain* (v. 11). The illustration of Cain (Genesis 4:1-13) is somewhat more difficult to interpret. It is quite widely held that Cain failed to bring a blood sacrifice to God and that because of that his sacrifice was not accepted. That usual interpretation may result from reading too much into the text, however. When we read of the various sacrifices demanded by Jehovah later, we learn that both vegetable and animal sacrifices were required (Leviticus 2-7). Vegetables (or grain) were required as expressions of thanks, whereas animal sacrifices were made for sins of various kinds. C. F. Keil comments that Abel's offering was accepted because it came from the heart.[1] Cain's offering was rejected because he was simply trying to keep on good terms with God. Keil believes that Abel brought the best of his flocks, whereas Cain offered vegetables but not the "firstfruits." Abel put his heart into his gift. Cain did not. Abel really believed God when he came with his sacrifice. Cain did not. Abel was reverent. Cain was not. That interpretation may well be correct, and it casts Hebrews 11:4 in a somewhat different light: "By faith Abel offered to God a better sacrifice than Cain, through which he obtained the testimony that he was righteous, God testifying about his gifts, and through faith, though he is dead, he still speaks."

The sacrifice of Abel was better because, in a real sense, he really believed God and "put his heart" into what he was doing. Cain went through with his sacrifice but not out of real faith and regard for the Person, commandments, and worship of God. That was the "way of Cain."

OUR IRREVERENT WORLD

Irreverence was a fundamental aspect of man's original sin. Paul writes: "For even though they knew God, they did not honor Him as God, or give thanks; but they became futile in their speculations, and their foolish heart was darkened. Professing to be wise, they became fools." So, man was unholy, impious, and irreverent almost from the beginning. He knew God. But he did not glorify Him or thank Him. Putting God out of his consciousness, he made idols and worshiped them instead.

Tribal peoples today sacrifice to the spirits but have little to do with the Creator God even though they often believe He exists. If you were to ask why they worship spirits but do not worship the Creator God, they would say that the spirits are close at hand but the Creator God is far away and does not bother them.

Similarly, modern man has pushed God farther and farther away from himself and his world. It was not so at the beginning of the scientific era. Alfred North Whitehead, Karl Oppenheimer, Francis Schaeffer, and many others stress the fact that science was born in a Christian awareness. Galileo, Copernicus, Francis Bacon, Johannes Kepler, and most scientists up to and including Isaac Newton believed in God. Schaeffer quotes Francis Bacon: "Man by the Fall fell at the same time from his state of innocence and from his dominion over nature. Both of these losses, however, can even in this life be in some part repaired; the former by religion and faith, the latter by the arts and sciences."[2] He also says: "Galileo stressed the fact that, when he looked at the universe in all its riches and its beauty (he did not mean merely aesthetic beauty but its unity in the midst of its complexity), he was called to only one end—to worship the beauty of the Creator."[3]

But belief in God gave way to belief in man. Theism gradually gave way to humanism. Theology was transformed into anthropology. Paul Vitz says that the most important source of this change was Ludwig Feuerbach's *Essence of Christianity,* first published in 1841.[4] In that book Feuerbach wrote, "That which in religion ranks first—namely, God—is . . . in truth and reality something second; for God is merely the projected essence of Man. What, therefore ranks second in religion—namely, Man—that must be proclaimed the first and recognized as the first."[5]

Thinkers influenced by Feuerbach include Friedrich Engels, Karl

Marx, Friedrich Nietzsche, Thomas Huxley, John Stuart Mill, Sigmund Freud, and John Dewey.[6]

Friedrich Nietzsche became the first to declare that God is dead. In *Thus Spoke Zarathustra* he has Zarathustra spend ten years on a mountain and then come down to preach this message: God is dead. Overman (Superman) is virtuous when he frees himself from belief in God. To worship is to return to childhood. If men must worship, let them worship a donkey.[7]

In a thousand ways and throughout his various pursuits, the modern worldling echoes Nietzsche. At his worst man's speech is riddled with profanity, and he shakes his fist at God. For example, one of the characters in James Baldwin's play *Blues for Mr. Charlie* says: "God . . . He can have his icy, snow-white heaven! If he is somewhere around this fearful planet, if I ever see him, I will spit in his face! In God's face! How dare he presume to judge a living soul!"[8] What insufferable blasphemy. What unbridled irreverence. What intolerable insolence. Man turns his back on God, plunders and pollutes his planet, rapes and murders his fellows—and then he blames God for his plight. The incomprehensible mystery is not that God "presumes to judge" but that He withholds His judgment for even a single second.

But that is not all. There is something almost as frightfully irreverent about seeing all that is still good and beautiful and pleasing in the world and ignoring the God who made it that way. To enjoy the beauty of the mountain; to delight in the kaleidoscopic colors of a sunset; to feel the velvet floor of the woods beneath one's feet; to indulge in the full-chorded harmony of a symphony—to experience all of that and yet to disregard the God who gave it. How irreverent. And how characteristic of our contemporary world.

IRREVERENCE IN THE CHURCH

The Christian who is contemporary (in the good sense of that word) is saddened by what is going on in the world, but he is not surprised by it. The surprise—or shall we say shock—comes with the realization of the extent to which the irreverence of the world has invaded the Church. Fueled by a basic unbelief (one of our university professors said that skepticism is so widespread among the clergy that skeptics should wear identifying lapel buttons to signal that in their presence a pretense of faith is unnecessary), irreverence in some form is apparent in the majority of Christian assemblies. It can be found in the attitude, words, and behavior of those who call themselves Christians.

OVERT, BLATANT IRREVERENCE

Examples of blatant irreverence are not hard to find. Consider the following:

• In the Sidney Carter song entitled "Friday Morning" a co-victim of Christ, who is also enroute to the place of crucifixion, echoes the sentiments of many unbelieving cynics. In words too blasphemous to quote here, he blames the crucifixion and the ills of the whole world on God, finally saying, "It's God they ought to crucify."[9]

• Rejecting protests, the dean of the famous St. Paul's in London, the Very Reverend Martin Sullivan invited the cast of the immoral musical *Hair* to participate in a special Sunday evening Communion service. During the Communion service "the old cathedral rocked to the thunder of 'The Age of Aquarius' and 'Three Five Zero Zero.' "[10]

• As part of a Communion service in New York's St. Clement's Episcopal Church, barefoot and blindfolded participants descended to the basement for confession and then symbolically flushed their sins away in the toilets.[11]

• At a Presbyterian Church (US) sponsored youth conference in Atlanta, young people were encouraged to write "succinct *graffiti*" expressing their feelings on panels located in the front of the room. That was followed by a "worship service" focused on obscenities.[12]

• About the time of the end of the war in Vietnam, Harvey Cox, author of *The Secular City* and professor at Harvard Divinity School, led a celebration of Easter designed to express his "theology of fantasy, festivity and celebration." According to *Newsweek,* it was an all-night affair, held in a discotheque in a converted warehouse, and attended by "hundreds of students, hippies, straights, blacks, whites, artists and clergymen." Among other things, the program featured a rock band called the "Apocrypha," dancing, Cox and other clerics in psychedelic robes, the reading of the resurrection account, and Handel's "Hallelujah" chorus. People fed each other bread and wine. Bright balloons were released and rose to the ceiling. At sunrise the crowd rushed outside, chanting, "Sun, sun, sun."[13]

COVERT, INCIPIENT IRREVERENCE

Of course, most forms of irreverence in the Church are more subtle. Consider the following illustrations, some of which are admittedly borderline cases.

• Attempts to be "culturally respectable" or "relevant" often lead to what D. G. Kehl calls "religious doublespeak."[14] The influence of Madison Avenue is apparent in such phrases as "Things go better with Christ"; "Honk if you love Jesus"; "You've got a lot to live and Jesus has a lot to give"; "Relief's just a prayer away"; and "Try Him—you'll like Him." Such doublespeak is characterized by an incongruity between what is said and what really is. It tends to obscure, distort, and misrepresent. It leaves the strong impression that Christ is a "religious tranquilizer" instead of the Lord of the universe and that God's grace is a sale item in a salvation franchise.

• A youth organization decides that the best way to appeal to today's young people is to adopt their language and life-style insofar as feasible. Their meetings are punctuated by expressions that come as close to profanity as possible without crossing some arbitrary line. God the Father is the "big guy in the sky," and Christ the Savior is "my pal, Jesus." Prayer abruptly interrupts any inane activity or dialogue and is engaged in while attendees flop on the floor or are draped over available furniture.

• For years everything goes along well for a certain believer. He takes his good fortune as evidence of the fact that God is good. Suddenly, the believer is beset by a series of misfortunes. His world crumbles around him. He refuses to believe that God has his good or the good of anyone else in mind in allowing such trials. He has exulted in the patient endurance of other suffering Christians, but he cannot accept suffering himself. He grumbles and complains that God is unfair, or worse.

• A congregation gathers for "worship" with a crescendo of conversation that reaches almost deafening proportions and can be broken off only by the persistent prodding of a patient pastor. About one hour later (woe be to those responsible for prolonging the worship service!) it becomes apparent that worship was but an interlude. After the solemnity of a biblical exposition and a final benediction, the temporary truce expires, spiritual exhortations are dismissed, and the sanctuary becomes alive with the resumption of conversation and frivolities. After all, the worshipers are true Christians, and any informality is allowable by virtue of the "beauty of holiness."

• Another congregation enters their sanctuary quietly and with seeming reverence. There is something inspiring and almost sanctifying about the brilliant rays falling on the stained-glass windows and the majestic chords flowing from the pipe organ. The service proceeds in accordance with a carefully prepared and wholly predictable pattern, every movement and word orchestrated so as to appeal to the senses and spirits of the worshipers. At the close of the service people quietly file out of the sanctuary and into the narthex, where some greet the robed pastor, many exchange brief greetings, and most rather quickly depart to attend to more engaging concerns—their duty to Jehovah accomplished for another week or two. Though they would have preferred other pursuits they have, after all, worshiped. For that they feel better, and they feel justified in whatever else they might choose to do. All has been transformed by the "holiness of beauty."

Many (perhaps most) of us have a tendency to come to a "worship service" with a focus on ourselves—our needs, desires, likes, and dislikes. Let us remember, the primary question in worship is not the frequently asked, "What have *we* gotten out of worship?" but the seldom asked, "What has *God* gotten out of worship?" We worship God because of who He is and because of what He desires and requires.

CONCLUSION

There is not a *world* of difference between the overt and covert forms of irreverence illustrated above. The same "world" is largely responsible for both forms. But there *is* a difference between them. Not many *overt* blasphemers will be disposed to read Jude—or to heed him if they do—even though they may be in the Church and bear the name *Christian*. Those who have been overtaken by one or more of the *covert* forms of irreverence, on the other hand, are far more likely to want to hear and heed the apostle. In all probability they are real Christians who have been unduly influenced by the world around them. Their spirits need a new consciousness of the Person of God.

In another context one of the authors has written of an experience with Dr. P. Krishna (a recent convert from Hinduism), which informed his own conscience with respect to irreverence.

Some years ago we sat together with a chapel audience addressed by an American youth evangelist. The evangelist's leather jacket, festooned with Jesus buttons, constituted a somewhat different attire for a seminary chapel. But it was the message itself which was most unique, punctuated as it was with references to Christ as a "great guy" and "good fellow," and delivered in rapid-fire style with no sense of awe or mystery. After a closing "Amen," I waited for Dr. Krishna to rise, but he just sat there, his head buried in his hands. Aware of his physical problems, I made inquiry. Slowly he lifted his head and, haltingly, said: "I just can't believe it. Is this the way Christians speak of the Lord of the universe?"[15]

The world is too much with us. Perhaps we must learn from those who, after long pilgrimages, have finally come to faith in the true God. Perhaps the newness of their awareness of who God is, and the freshness of their faith in His Person and power, will remind us that God, after all, is God.

NOTES

1. C. F. Keil and F. Delitzsch, *Commentary on the Old Testament,* Vol. 1, *The Pentateuch* (Grand Rapids: Eerdmans, 1949), pp. 110-11.

2. Francis Schaeffer, *The Church at the End of the Twentieth Century* (Downers Grove, Ill.: Inter-Varsity, 1970), p. 9.
3. Ibid.
4. Paul Vitz, *Psychology as Religion: The Cult of Self-Worship* (Grand Rapids: Eerdmans, 1977, p. 67.
5. Quoted in ibid., p. 68.
6. Ibid., p. 67.
7. Friedrich Nietzsche, *Thus Spake Zarathustra,* trans. Thomas Common (New York: Random House, The Modern Library, n.d.), pp. 352-56.
8. James Baldwin, "Blues for Mister Charlie," in Clinton F. Oliver and Stephanie Sills, eds., *Contemporary Black Drama* (New York: Scribner's, 1971), p. 297.
9. Cited by Vernon C. Grounds in "Is the Church a Cultural Fossil?" *Christian Heritage,* January 1970, p. 6. See Carlton R. Young, *Songbook for Saints and Sinners* (Chicago: Agape, 1971).
10. Raymond R. Coffey, "Cathedral Survives 'Hair' Fallout," *Chicago Daily News,* 2 December 1971.
11. "Church Panorama," *Christianity Today,* 14 February 1969, p. 44.
12. "Obscenity in the Church," *Christianity Today,* 31 January 1969, p. 27.
13. Quoted in Andrew Greeley, *Unsecular Man* (New York: Schocken Books, 1972), pp. 164-65.
14. D. G. Kehl, "Have You Committed Verbicide Today?" *Christianity Today,* 27 January 1978, p. 18.
15. David J. Hesselgrave, *Communicating Christ Cross-Culturally* (Grand Rapids: Zondervan, 1978, p. 171.

5

SENSUALITY—THE SIN OF THE BODY

For certain persons have crept in unnoticed, those who were long beforehand marked out for this condemnation, ungodly persons who turn the grace of our God into licentiousness.

JUDE 4

INTRODUCTION

Look on the shelves of almost any bookstore, secular or religious, and you will find expanding space being given to the interests of a sensate culture. Rest assured, however, that though contemporary tastes and the flare for explicitness result in a glut of literature (and films, art, and music) appealing to the natural senses, the exploitation of those interests is not new. It was evident in the world of Jude's day and long before that. What sent Jude scurrying for his pen was the realization that in the persons of some scurrilous apostates that aspect of worldly culture had also found its way into the churches.

JUDE ON SENSUALITY

Return to verse 4. Jude writes that the people he has in mind change the grace (*charis*) of God into sensuality (*aselgeia*).

What is *charis*? The standard answer is that grace is the unmerited favor of God. And that it is. But it is more than that. It also refers to a thankful acceptance of God's favor. In grace there is a reciprocal relationship. God gives His good gifts and then receives the thankful praise of men who accept and appreciate those gifts.

	Irreverence	*Sensuality*
Designation	*Asebeia*—ungodliness, impiety, irreverence (v. 4)	*Aselgeia*—license for immorality, sensuality (v. 4)
Explanations and descriptions	1. "Revile angelic majesties" 2. "Revile [speak abusively]" (v. 10) 3. "Ungodly deeds which they have done" (v. 15) 4. "Grumblers, finding fault" (v. 16) 5. "Mockers" (v. 18)	1. "By dreaming, defile the flesh" (v. 8) 2. Destroyed by "things . . . they know by instinct" (v. 10) 3. "Following after their own lusts" (v. 16) 4. "Flattering . . . for advantage" (v. 16) 5. "Worldly-minded" (v. 19)
Metaphors and analogies	"Hidden reefs in your love feasts" (v. 12)	1. "Caring for [only] themselves" (v. 12) 2. "Clouds without water, carried along by winds" (v. 12) 3. "Autumn trees without fruit . . . uprooted" (v. 12) 4. "Wild waves of the sea" (v. 13)
Precursors and examples	1. The people of the Exodus (v. 5) 2. Michael the archangel (v. 9) 3. The way of Cain (v. 11)	1. Sodom and Gomorrah (v. 7) 2. Balaam's error (v. 11)

There is a sense in which grace is not complete until man responds appropriately to God's beneficence. That is why it has been customary in some traditions to refer to table prayers as "grace." Thankful reception is part and parcel of the word *charis*. What, then, is *aselgeia?* The translators have had a difficult time with that word, variously translating it as lasciviousness, wantonness, licentiousness, license, immorality, and sensuality, or as a combination of those words. William Barclay says that it involves a loss of shame, sinning and not caring.[1] But it is not just any kind of sin that is in view. In the New Testament, *aselgeia* is related to the sins of *greed, self-indulgence and sexual immorality*. Note that those are *body*-centered, *flesh*-oriented and *self*-gratifying. In other words, they are forms of sensuality.

That Jude is thinking in those terms becomes evident as one examines his letter further.

EXPLANATIONS AND DESCRIPTIONS

Jude expands on his meaning in the following ways:

• These people are dreamers who "pollute [*miainō*] their own bodies" (v. 8). The word means to dye, stain, or pollute. Ultimately sensuality degrades that in which it initially delighted.

• They are being destroyed by things that they *instinctively* understand (v. 10). For all their pretended knowledge, what they really know is what dumb animals know, and in those animal appetites they corrupt themselves.

• "They follow their own evil desires" (v. 16, NIV).

• "They flatter others for their own advantage" (v. 16, NIV). Literally, they "admire faces." This is a most descriptive Hebraism, which can be used in a good or bad sense. Here it is used in a bad sense. Alfred Plummer says that these people were "courtiers, flatterers and parasites."[2] Why do they do it? Because by courting the right people they add to their own prestige, prosperity, and power.

• They "follow mere natural instincts and do not have the Spirit" (v. 19). Jude's word is *psuchikoi* (the "sensual, fleshly ones"). That is what early "proto-Gnostics" said *others* were. They themselves claimed to be the *pneumatikoi,* or the "spiritual ones." And, being "spiritual people" who had received divine grace, they believed themselves to be free to indulge in bodily appetites.

By way of example, one exponent of an incipient Gnosticism was Menander, a disciple of Simon Magus, who apparently made a significant impact in Asia Minor in the first century.[3] Simon Magus, whom we first encounter as an active opponent of Peter in Acts 8, taught that the law was a device originated by the angels to enslave men. Since men are saved by God's grace they are completely free from the restraints of the Law. To prove his point, he himself lived with a prostitute, whom he described as the "incarnate mother of all."[4]

Jude's appraisal of those "proto-Gnostics" was the reverse of their own. They divided mankind into two groups. They claimed that they were not *psuchikoi,* or sensual. Jude says they were. They claimed that they were *pneumatikoi,* or spiritual. Jude says they were devoid of the Spirit.

METAPHORS AND ANALOGIES

In addition to those explicit descriptions, some of the metaphors used by Jude seem to fit these people to a "T."

1. *"Shepherds who feed only themselves"* (v. 12, NIV). It is hard to imagine a shepherd whose only concern is that his own stomach be filled. Implicit in the very designation *shepherd* is the idea that he will care for the needs of the sheep. One recalls Jesus' dialogue with His errant disciple Peter. Three times Jesus queried, "Simon son of John, do you truly love me?" And three times Peter replied, "Yes, Lord, you know that I love you." Jesus said, "Feed my sheep" (John 21:15-17, NIV). At first Peter was miffed, but later he got the message: "To the elders among you, I appeal . . . be shepherds of God's flock . . . not greedy . . . but eager to serve . . ." (1 Peter 5:1-3, NIV). The leaders Jude has in mind were stuffing themselves while the sheep were starving.

2. *"Clouds without water, carried along by winds"* (v. 12). How descriptive. Imagine that you are a farmer surveying a field of grain. The stalks are just beginning to mature. But day after day the sky

has been cloudness. And now the sun is still hot, and the ground is parched. Without rain all will be lost. Then, in the distance, clouds begin to form. The wind begins to blow, bending the stalks of grain. The clouds roll over the fields. Rain, at last! But it is not to be. Hours later the wind is spent, the clouds have disappeared. And there is still no rain. That is a picture of false teachers. Carried by the winds of prevailing ideas, they put in their appearance and "do their thing." But after all is said and done, the water of life has been withheld. The people languish.

3. *"Autumn trees without fruit, doubly dead, uprooted"* (v. 12). It is fall. The pickers have worked their way through the orchards. But there are some trees that have not responded to nature and care. Consequently they have been pulled out of the ground, and, their roots exposed, they await the inevitable fire. What a contrast to the psalmist's picture of the man who loves and meditates on God's law: "He will be like a tree firmly planted by streams of water, which yields its fruit in its season and its leaf does not wither" (Psalm 1:3).

4. *"Wild waves of the sea, casting up their own shame"* (v. 13). Only those who live by the sea can fully appreciate this metaphor. The sea constantly yields its debris and consistently retains its treasures. The storm does not change but rather accentuates the process. So it is with apostasy and heresy. To the extent that they are tolerated, the Church becomes a shore littered with the shame of spent ideas and unsanctified behavior.

PRECURSORS AND EXAMPLES

Finally, Jude provides us with living examples of the sort of thing that he has in mind. There may be some warrant for thinking that the fallen angels mentioned in verse 6 were guilty of sensuality and immorality. If the "sons of God" mentioned in Genesis 6 were angels, as some believe, then their cohabitation with the "daughters of men" was a monstrous evil, and the fallen angels are examples of sensual living.

That interpretation is questionable however. The *clear* examples of sensuality are Sodom and Gomorrah and surrounding towns (v. 7) and Balaam (v. 11). Let us look at those more closely.

1. *Sodom, Gomorrah, and surrounding towns.* Jude says that the people of those cities and towns "indulged in gross immorality (v. 7). The reference is to Genesis 19. Lot was host to two angels in his house in Sodom. About the time they prepared to retire, men young and old from various parts of the city surrounded the house. They demanded that Lot deliver his guests over to their immoral purposes (Genesis 19:5). Lot tried to discourage his fellow townsmen from such evil acts, but so perverted were the Sodomites that they derided and threatened Lot. "This one came in as an alien, and already he is acting like a judge; now we will treat you worse than them," they replied (Genesis 19:9). The Sodomites were about to break down the door when they were struck blind—the darkness of their hearts culminating in the blindness of their eyes.

Sodom and Gomorrah were destroyed. But their infamous memory has survived the erasures of history. Today, the very names are synonymous with the worst forms of sensuality.

2. *Balaam.* Balaam is a rather clouded character in the Scriptures. One of the great messianic prophecies of Holy Writ was uttered by Balaam: "I see him, but not now; I behold him, but not near; a star shall come forth from Jacob, and a scepter shall rise from Israel" (Numbers 24:17).

But Jude speaks of Balaam's "error" (v. 11). What was it? To understand, we must determine what he did that was wrong. And then we must ask why he did it. The record is found in Numbers 22-24.

Balak, king of the Moabites, greatly respected Balaam's supernatural powers. Fearing that the Israelites would destroy Moab as they had destroyed the Amorites, Balak requested Balaam to come and put a curse on the newcomers from Egypt. Balaam inquired of the Lord what he should do. Then in obedience to the Lord, Balaam refused Balak's request.

When greater rewards were promised and Balaam inquired of the Lord a second time, God allowed him to go to Balak but was greatly displeased with him. Balaam was warned to speak only that which God told him. Three times Balaam blessed the Israelites. He was not to be bought with gold and silver. Bitterly disappointed, Balak sent him away.

But, unfortunately, the record does not end there. Camping close to the Moabites, the men of Israel first engaged in sexual immorality with the Moabite women and then joined them in the worship of Baal (Numbers 25:1-3). How did this happen? Evidently Balaam advised the Moabite women to seduce the children of Israel as a means of bringing divine judgment upon the chosen people (Numbers 31:15). It seems that greed and self-indulgence finally got the best of Balaam, and lust got the best of Israel. In the end, he who had said, "Let me die the death of the upright, and let my end be like his" (Numbers 23:10) died with the idolators at the command of Moses (Numbers 31:7-8).

Our interpretation of Balaam's sin is reinforced by John's letter to the church at Pergamum (Revelation 2:12-17). John writes that Balaam "kept teaching Balak to put a stumbling block before the sons of Israel, to eat food sacrificed to idols, and to commit acts of immorality" (Revelation 2:14).

But John does more than interpret the "teaching of Balaam." He relates it to the teaching of the Nicolaitans and insists that there are those in the church who hold to that doctrine. It is interesting to note in this connection that Nicolaos ("conqueror of the people") is thought to be a Greek version of the Hebrew name *Balaam* ("destroyer of the people"). Little wonder that, in spite of the good things the Holy Spirit inspired John to write about the Pergamum church, He also caused John to add a warning: "You also have some who in the same way hold the teaching of the Nicolaitans. Repent therefore; or else I am coming to you quickly and I will make war against them with the sword of My mouth" (Revelation 2:15-16).

OUR SENSUAL WORLD

Enter, now, the twentieth century. Could any time in history be more sensual than our own time?

CONTEMPORARY PHILOSOPHY AND PSYCHOLOGY

Think of prominent emphases in contemporary philosophy. Naturalism has presumed that this world is all there is. The Creator has been wrenched away. The Fall has been discounted. Man reigns supreme in nature. Nature reigns supreme in man. What is "natural" is good—naturally!

Materialism has prized that which is tangible. It has disparaged the spiritual. Laws governing the production and distribution of material goods are now determinative for social systems. The employment of material goods to promote creature comforts is a way of life.

Humanism has placed man at the center of the universe. That is really the subject of the next chapter, but it is important to note here that man himself has become the measure of all things.

Much of the contemporary psychology also reflects and reinforces those philosophies. Psychology in the Western world is characterized by a pervasive "selfism." That is typified in the following statement by Carl Rogers: "Unconditional self regard occurs when the client perceives himself in such a way that no self experience can be discriminated as more or less worthy of positive regard as any other."[5]

In a word, philosophy and psychology have turned things upside down. Nature takes precedence over supernature; the material replaces the spiritual; man preempts the place of God.

CONTEMPORARY LIFE-STYLE

The hallmarks of our day are greed, self-indulgence, and immorality—often disguised as "success," "the good life," and "love." True, to be successful does not necessarily mean that one is greedy. Granted, one can enjoy life without being self-indulgent. Agreed, sex is not synonymous with sin. But consider the contemporary life-style in terms of the ways in which it translates those motivations into action.

1. *Greed.* It seems unnecessary to call attention to the degree that greed has pervaded national life in America. The urge to "get ahead" and to get more and more lies behind many of the demands made upon government, unfair pricing on the part of management, and the voracious appetite of labor unions for higher and higher wages and increased benefits. All of that at the cost of runaway inflation and the well-being of future generations.

2. *Self-indulgence.* Speaking of "selfism's" relation to consumerism, Paul Vitz says, "Selfism's clear advocacy of experience now, and not inhibiting or repressing, was a boon to the advertising industry. . . . Most of the short expressions and catch words of self theory make excellent advertising copy: Do it now! Have a new experience! Honor thyself!"[6] No wonder American society has, unashamedly, become the user of an inordinate amount of the world's resources. Although Americans make up only 5.6 percent of the world's population, we consume 42 percent of the world's aluminum, 33 percent of its copper, 44 percent of its coal, 33 percent of its petroleum, and 63 percent of its natural gas.[7] No wonder that beer, wine, and liquors flow like water in our society. There are approximately 10 million problem drinkers (some say 17 million) in the United States; an estimated 3.3 million of them are among young people in the 14 to 17 age category.[8] And all of this is supposed to constitute the "good life." Evidently only economic reality will change us.

3. *Immorality.* But perhaps it is in the area of sexual immorality that the sensuality of our age is most apparent. It seems but yesterday that the prophet and apostle of sensuality D. H. Lawrence challenged our moral code with his *Lady Chatterly's Lover.* That book met with challenge after challenge in schools and courts. But it was a losing battle. The floodgates were opened. Pornographic literature and movies became commonplace. First, Alfred Kinsey analyzed and publicized America's most intimate sexual behavior patterns. Then William Masters and Virginia Johnson introduced bizarre sexual "therapy." Finally, in a book entitled *Open Marriage—A New Lifestyle for Couples,* George and Nena O'Neill advocated extramarital sex as a way of keeping marriages intact and "healthy."[9]

Amidst much discussion and controversy, sex education has now been introduced into our educational system. But without a common source for moral values and with a bias against "imposing a teacher's values upon a student," sex education turns out to be little more than an adventure into human biology, instruction in contraceptive methods, and antidotes for venereal disease.

America now begins to reap its bitter harvest. More than a million American teenagers—30,000 of them fourteen years of age or younger—become pregnant every year.[10] At least one million abortions are performed in America every year.[11] Almost half of our marriages end in the divorce courts. Homosexuals press for "equal rights" so that their life-style will be legitimized and they will be free to teach our children.

Perhaps a recent book and an arresting billboard say it all. The book is Frederick J. Streng, Charles L. Lloyd, Jr., and J. T. Allen's *Ways of Being Religious* in which the "enjoyment of the full life through sensuous experiences" is proposed as a way of being religious.[12] The billboard stood for long weeks atop a large office building near Chicago's O'Hare International Airport. There it emblazoned its message in neon lights across the sky: "IF IT FEELS GOOD—DO IT!"

"THE CRISIS OF OUR AGE"

In his classic work of a generation ago entitled *The Crisis of Our Age,* Harvard sociologist Pitirim A. Sorokin describes three systems of truth: ideational, idealistic, and sensate. He describes ideational truth as *the truth of faith,* truth revealed by the grace of God through His mouthpieces and in a supersensory way. Sensate truth, he says, is *the truth of the senses* obtained through our organs of sense perception. Idealistic truth is a synthesis of both, made by reason— reason that recognizes the role of the sense organs in determining truth concerning sensory phenomena and of God's revelation in determining the truth of supersensory phenomena. Sorokin believes that each source of knowledge—senses, intuition, and reason—has its place and that the viable society recognizes all three.

According to Sorokin, the crisis in Western society consists in precisely this: Western society has become committed to one system of truth—sensory truth—a system within which are to be found poisons that have now increased to lethal proportions. Decadent Western society is at the crossroads. It must recover revelation and reason or pass into oblivion.

Sorokin does not give evidence of being a Christian in the biblical sense of that word. But, in some respects, that makes his analysis even more significant. In any case, to a degree almost unparalleled in the work of twentieth-century social historians, Sorokin pinpoints the ills of our sensate culture. Attend to some of his words:

> . . . in a sensate society natural science replaces religion, theology, and even speculative philosophy. . . . A fully developed sensate system of truth and cognition is inevitably *materialistic,* viewing everything, openly or covertly, in its materialistic aspects. . . . Society becomes economically minded and the "economic interpretation of history" begins to hold undisputed sway. . . . Anything spiritual, supersensory or idealistic is ridiculed, being replaced by the most degrading and debasing interpretations. . . . If reality is sensory . . . what could be more sensory . . . than matter, and what could be more real than reflexes, digestive functions, sex and so on? . . . A further consequence of such a system of truth is the development of a *temporalistic, relativistic, and nihilistic mentality.* . . . Hence . . . , as tomorrow is uncertain; snatch the present kiss; get rich quick; seize the power, popularity, fame, and opportunity of the moment, because only present values can be grasped. . . . Everything becomes relative—truth and error, moral and aesthetic considerations and what not. A thing may be good today and bad tomorrow. . . . Sooner or later, relativism gives place to skepticism, cynicism, and nihilism. . . . No society can long exist under these conditions.[13]

Sorokin has proved himself to be a most perceptive analyst of Western society. Contemporary observers such as Philip Rieff are echoing the analysis he made a generation ago. According to Rieff we have now entered a new period of history, dominated by psychologizers who intend to reconstruct society on the basis of the principle of "impulse release." Our society is controlled by the urge to satisfy "an infinite variety of wants raised to the status of needs." The religious man who is born to be saved is thus rapidly being replaced by the psychological man who is born to be pleased. And with this change, guilt has been converted into "the sense of guilt" and thrown on the trash heap of neurotic behavior.[14] Such is the mentality conveyed by popular magazines like *Cosmopolitan,* which promises its readers that "you can become the sexual aggressor, have a great time, and not feel guilty afterward; you can transform yourself from victimized virgin to sultry seductress."[15]

The question is, How can the Church turn its world back to God and eternal values? The answer is that it must first recognize the extent to which a sensate world has invaded the Church and revive eternal values in its fellowship.

SENSUALITY AND THE CHURCH

We have already noted how first-century Gnosticism unlocked the doors of many early churches to sensuality. Down through the history of the Church many individuals and movements have perpetrated the Gnostics ethos—the Manicheans, the Catharists, the "Free Spirit," and the Ranter, to name a few. The "Free Spirit," for example, flourished in Europe in the fourteenth century and taught that humanity is composed of two groups—the "crude in spirit" (the majority) and the "subtle in Spirit." Only the latter have the potential of being wholly transformed into God. And the surest mark of such a transformation is a release from the sense of sin and the consequent ability to indulge in promiscuity without qualms of conscience.[16] The doctrines of the "Free Spirit" persisted into the sixteenth and seventeenth centuries and were the object of frequent attacks by the reformers Martin Luther and John Calvin.[17]

In part, the teachings of the "Free Spirit" also found expression in the theology of the Ranter of the seventeenth century, who justified immoral conduct on the grounds that "all things are Christ's" and that "to the pure, all things are pure."

History as well as Scripture, therefore, reminds us of the enormous capacity of professing Christians for self-deception. But how is it with the Church today? Obviously the Church has not transformed the world. Has the world transformed the Church?

OVERT AND BLATANT SENSUALITY IN THE CHURCH

1. *Greed and self-indulgence.* From the point of view of the man on the street the most unvarnished evidence of self-indulgence on the part of church people lies in the similarity between their life-

style and that of nonchurch people. Indeed, in an affluent society it is not easy to demonstrate Christian "otherliness" by the homes in which we live, the cars we drive, the clothes we wear, and the food we eat. But upon closer examination, the lives of even prosperous Christians should evidence a certain generosity and concern for others that is largely absent in the world. Unfortunately the message and life-style of some church people give worldlings reason to point to the Church in derision.

Consider, for example, the message and life-style of "Reverend Ike," who promises his followers success, prosperity, and "anything they want" if they will but follow his teachings and contribute to his church. A typical advertisement of one of his meetings tells it all:

Success and Prosperity
can be yours
right here and
right NOW!

Surround yourself with
all the good you desire. . . .

Health—Happiness—Love
Success—Prosperity—Money. . . .

Message:
"How to be Rich in Every Way!"[18]

On his radio programs, Reverend Ike's guests are called upon for testimonials as to how they "got what they wanted." A typical testimonial came from one couple who told how they had always wanted the biggest and best-equipped Cadillac. After hearing Reverend Ike and following his directions they went to the Cadillac dealer and made a downpayment. They were able to make the payments, and now the Cadillac is theirs—along with the money to operate it!

2. *Immorality.* Lamentably, even immorality is condoned by some sections of the institutional church. The Unitarian Universalist Association has introduced a sex education program for children (aged 12-14) in about half of its 1,100 Sunday schools. The program includes movies of adults engaging in explicit heterosexual and

homosexual acts. The children are encouraged to discuss sex in street terms rather than polite language so they will "feel at home" in Sunday school.

Recently the United Methodist Church's General Board of Discipline approved the use of sexually explicit films in the training of leaders for church sponsored seminars in sex education. Its reasoning was that such films would be helpful in giving "an understanding of the full range of human sexual practice."[19]

Following a decision by the (US) Episcopal Church's House of Bishops that it is inappropriate to ordain a practicing homosexual, the parent Church of England published a report urging fundamental changes in attitudes toward homosexuals and recommending that they *not* be barred from the priesthood.[20]

The much publicized Universal Fellowship of Metropolitan Churches claims to believe in salvation by faith in Christ alone while wholeheartedly endorsing the gay life-style. The mother church attained a membership of approximately 1,000 and founded some 110 congregations in seven countries with a combined membership of 67,000—all within a span of about ten years.[21] One member of the church commented that when someone has a problem "nothing is more powerful than a church full of fairies praying."

COVERT AND INCIPIENT SENSUALITY IN THE CHURCH

In most cases, that which Jude terms *aselgeia* comes in a more subtle form. Let us examine some of the ways in which our sensate culture may be invading the Church and our own life-styles. Note that we do not label all the following phenomena "sensual" necessarily. We only say that they have that potential. Carried too far, or in the wrong direction, even the most noble of truths and the most desirable of programs may serve the flesh rather than the Spirit.

1. *Greed.* Of course we would not *call* it greed. The word is seldom used in the world or in the Church anymore. But in the few quiet, reflective moments that we as Christians entertain in these days of unparalleled activism, does it not sometimes seem that the desire for bigger and better churches, higher and more prestigious titles and positions, and larger and larger paychecks may be greediness?

Of course, God wants His Church to grow. And we need some larger churches that will become the bases for city-wide or even nationwide ministries. But God does not want the Church to grow at any cost. If my church (or mission or institution) grows at the expense of other Christ-honoring churches, or if the message is changed in order to make it more appealing to the audience, then the growth of my church is an affront to God. Moreover, sometimes the church should grow by designed division—planting new churches in needy communities. The Lord of the Church wants more churches, not just bigger churches.

Clergy and laity alike may be afflicted with the desire for prestigious titles and positions. The desire for unearned or half-earned academic degrees, the aspiration to be the senior pastor (this implies a pastoral staff) or the president or the director, the tendency to prize social position more than godliness in electing members of boards—all those and more *may* constitute evidence of pride and greed. In any case, we Christians need to rethink our value systems.

Of course, everyone wants, and most get, larger and larger paychecks. In fact, inflation has become so much a part of the system that salary increases are necessary in order to keep pace. But, again, we Christians need to ask ourselves some serious questions. Is it ever in order for those whose affections are not to be set on things on earth (Colossians 3:1) to say, "That's enough. We don't need more"? Again, does our generosity match our prosperity? Are we really *stewards* of our possessions?

2. *Self-indulgence.* First, we must ask ourselves whether we have preached the whole counsel of God. As Christ's disciples we are called upon to deny ourselves and follow Him (Matthew 16:24). Faithful teaching and preaching emphasize the cost of discipleship. Therefore it is incumbent upon us to make an evaluation of our teaching and preaching. Do we preach both Christ's cross *and* the believer's cross? Do we teach that just as Jesus shares our burdens so we should bear one another's burdens? What about the "positive gospel" that neglects themes like repentance and judgment and preaches an easy believism? What about the insistence that the Christian life is the most exciting, happy, and self-fulfilling life imaginable? Are those truths or half-truths?

Second, we must inquire into the inordinate attention given to experience in some church circles. Consider, for example, the sponsors of an interdenominational conference who invited Christian clergy and lay persons of all denominations and backgrounds to "leave doctrine at home" and come together to seek a spiritual experience that would transcend all differences and unite participants in the Holy Spirit. What kind of comment is that upon the Holy Spirit-inspired Scriptures, which alone constitute the standard for true doctrine and authentic spiritual experience? Or, consider the recent Gallup poll showing that 31 million American adults indicate that they are evangelicals, while only six in ten of those can correctly identify "Ye must be born again" as the words of Jesus to Nicodemus.[22] Must we not rethink a one-sided, feelings-oriented, experience-based Christianity that downgrades doctrine and neglects the Bible? Is conversion no more than some ill-defined religious experience? Is the Christian life only a succession of "spiritual highs"? Or is much of the foregoing simply another form of self-indulgence?

Third, it is incumbent upon us to examine our life-style. It is true that God "richly supplies us with all things to enjoy" (1 Timothy 6:17). The line between enjoying God's good gifts and self-indulgence may sometimes seem to be a fine line, but it is a very real one. A well-known evangelist invited a number of friends to a restaurant in a large midwestern city. When all were seated the waitress gave each one a menu, whereupon the evangelist said, "My friends, do not hesitate to order anything you desire. Remember, God's servants deserve the very best." If this is so, why must tens of thousands of the most elite of God's family be grateful for the most simple fare? Do we require the best because we are "Christianized" or because we are "enculturated"?

5. *Immorality.* The incipient forms of immorality in the Church are advanced on two bases: "redefinition" and "reaffirmation."

Liberalism has "demythologized" Christian terminology to fit the philosophy of modern potential psychology. Sin in that theological framework basically means that which frustrates my self-actualization; grace is that which offers deliverance from my personal predicament; and divine love means total and unconditional acceptance of what one is. When combined with situation ethics, which makes "love" the only norm, this approach leads to a total "redefinition" of morality not unlike that advocated by many secularists.

According to a United Church of Christ study, the rightness or wrongness of sexual behavior should be determined by whether or not it contributes to human fulfillment and wholeness.[23] According to a study of human sexuality sponsored by the Catholic Theological Society of America, the Bible should not be understood as giving absolute prescriptions in regard to sex. Rather, sexual acts need to be evaluated in terms of whether or not they are honest, faithful, joyous, life-serving, self-liberating, socially responsible, and enriching for others. On that basis chastity becomes "that virtue which enables a person to transform the power of human sexuality into an integrative force in his or her life . . . and facilitates the fullest realization of one's being male or female and encourages the integration of self with others in the human community."[24]

That leads to the absurd conclusion that the hours a man spends with his lover can be "true" and "good," whereas the nights spent with an unloved wife are "sinful" and "bad." Similarly, the morality of homosexuality is to be determined by the "intent" of the actor, not the act itself. If homosexual practice is intended to express love (and not promiscuity) as part of an ongoing, permanent relationship, it is morally good.[25]

That is little more than a baptism of the secular redefinition of love as applying to all acts of passion. But it can be compelling. And it has left its mark in evangelical circles. Not long ago the teacher of a young people's Sunday school class in an evangelical Chicago church argued persuasively that the sanctity of the act of sex does not depend on a sheet of paper issued by the state or even on a ritual performed by the Church, but solely upon the genuine love for, and sincere commitment to, another person.

A closely related basis of immorality is "reaffirmation." That approach to questions of sex disdains outmoded Victorian ideas and reaffirms that sex is the gift of God and that the act of marriage is divinely ordained. So far so good. But exponents often proceed from there to explicitly describe and implicitly condone all kinds of sexual behavior. One employs the language and techniques of harlotry to "enhance" the marriage relationship, encouraging wives to periodically "seduce" their husbands under the dining room table.[26] Of course, whatever misgivings one might have with that advice, its virtue is that it is addressed to marriage partners.

But consider the case of formerly married Christian singles in a large California church. Only 9 percent of the men and 27 percent of the women have remained celibate in their single state. Of 203 singles interviewed, over one-fourth of them rationalized their sexual conduct by affirming that "Christ wants us to live abundant lives; to me that includes sex." Peer group pressure upon the minority who remained celibate moved one to comment, "I believe and practice celibacy, but in America in the 1970's I have to hide this fact even from church people."[27]

CONCLUSION

It has wisely been said that old errors never die, they just assume new forms. The world has given an entirely new form to the ageless error that says that man's problem is something other than sin. W. T. Jones, for example, comments,

> ... the first thing that strikes the modern reader of the *Confessions* is Augustine's extraordinary (or, as we might be inclined to say, "abnormal") sense of sin. By our standards, certainly, his childhood was remarkably blameless; yet to Augustine the escapades that we think of as normal products of youthful exuberance were signs of a diseased soul. ... .[28]

The leaders of the early Church turned this world upside down. Is the world turning the contemporary Church upside down? That certainly is a danger. And to the extent that we change the grace of God into a license for *aselgeia,* it is also a reality.

NOTES

1. William Barclay, *The Letters of John and Jude* (Philadelphia: Westminster, 1960), p. 180.
2. Charles John Ellicott, ed., *Ellicott's Commentary on the Whole Bible,* 8 vols. (Grand Rapids: Zondervan, 1954), "Introduction to the General Epistle of Jude," by Alfred Plummer, 8:513.

3. Walter Bauer, *Orthodoxy and Heresy in Earliest Christianity* (Philadelphia: Fortress, 1971), p. 66.
4. Edwin Yamauchi, *Gnostic Ethics and Mandean Origins* (Cambridge, Mass.: Harvard U. Press, 1970), p. 26.
5. Paul Vitz, *Psychology as Religion: The Cult of Self-Worship* (Grand Rapids: Eerdmans, 1977), p. 79.
6. Ibid., p. 62.
7. John V. Taylor, *Enough is Enough: A Biblical Call for Moderation in a Consumer* (Minneapolis: Augsburg, 1975), pp. 22-45.
8. Editorial, *The Evangelical Beacon,* 13 November 1979, p. 10.
9. George and Nena O'Neill, *Open Marriage: A New Lifestyle for Couples* (New York: Avon, 1972).
10. *Chicago Tribune,* 11 November 1979.
11. Harold O. J. Brown, *Abortion on Demand* (Washington, D.C.: Christian Action Council, n.d.).
12. Frederick J. Streng, Charles L. Lloyd, Jr., and Jay T. Allen, *Ways of Being Religious: Readings for a New Approach to Religion* (Englewood Cliffs, N.J.: Prentice-Hall, 1973), pp. 544-612. There is much within these pages with which we can agree. God has created all things to be enjoyed. But there is also much here that is, pure and simple, worldly philosophy.
13. Pitirim A. Sorokin, *The Crisis of Our Age: The Social and Cultural Outlook* (New York: Dutton, 1942), pp. 87-98 passim.
14. Philip Rieff, *Triumph of the Therapeutic* (New York: Harper & Row, 1967), pp. 17-21.
15. John Nelson, *Your God Is Alive and Well and Appearing in Popular Culture* (Philadelphia: Westminster, 1967), p. 20.
16. Norman Cohn, *The Pursuit of the Millennium* (New York: Oxford U. Press, 1970), p. 189.
17. Ibid., pp. 170-71.
18. David J. Hesselgrave, *Communicating Christ Cross-Culturally* (Grand Rapids: Zondervan, 1978), p. 425.
19. *Methodist Reporter,* 13 January 1980, p. 2.
20. *Chicago Tribune,* 19 October 1979.
21. Tim LaHaye, *The Unhappy Gays* (Wheaton: Tyndale, 1978), pp. 180-81.
22. "The Christianity Today—Gallup Poll: An Overview," *Christianity Today,* 21 December 1979, pp. 12-15.
23. Richard Lovelace, *Homosexuality and the Church* (Old Tappan, N.J.: Revell, 1978), p. 57.
24. Ibid., p. 55.
25. Richard Quebedeaux, *The Worldly Evangelicals* (New York: Harper & Row, 1973), p. 130.
26. Marabel Morgan, *The Total Woman* (Old Tappan, N.J.: Revell, 1973), p. 120.
27. Harold Ivan Smith, "Sex and Singleness the Second Time Around," *Christianity Today,* 25 May 1979, pp. 16-22.
28. W. T. Jones, *The Medieval Mind: A History of Western Philosophy,* 2d ed. (New York: Harcourt Brace Jovanovich, 1969), p. 75.

QUESTIONS FOR REFLECTION AND DISCUSSION

1. Covetousness basically means "wanting more and more" or "ruthless greed" and, in the New Testament, is often linked with both the desire for material gain and sexual lust (cf. Mark 7:21;

Colossians 3:5). When can enjoyment of material goods and sexual pleasure as gifts of God become "covetousness"? (See Isaiah 56:11; cf. Luke 12:14-34; Galatians 5:13; Philippians 4:11-12; Colossians 3:17; 1 Timothy 6:17.)

2. C. S. Lewis once remarked: "We are half-hearted creatures, fooling about with drink and sex and ambition when infinite joy is offered us, like an ignorant child who continues to go on making mud pies in a slum because he cannot imagine what is meant by the offer of a holiday at sea. We are far too easily pleased" (*The Weight of Glory* [Grand Rapids: Eerdmans, 1965], p. 2). Why is that often the case even for Christians who claim to believe in God's promise of reward?

3. Read 1 Corinthians 5. In what ways can indifference towards immorality on the part of leaders in the church be as serious as the actual involvement in sin? How is it that a church could actually be proud of such an attitude of indifference? How characteristic is that of churches today?

4. How would you respond to the individual who condones sex outside of marriage because "Christ wants us to live abundant lives"? How would you respond to the individual who justifies homosexual behavior because for some people it is a "natural" way of expressing oneself?

5. How does the Christian understanding of "success" differ from that of the world? What implications should this have for the jobs we seek, our life-styles, and the way in which we use our possessions? (See Matthew 20:25-28; 25:21; Luke 16:15; 1 Corinthians 13:1-3.) Reflect upon the following statement: "In Christianity, success is not measured by position as much as by disposition." Do you agree?

6

LAWLESSNESS—THE SIN OF THE SOUL

*For certain persons have crept in unnoticed, those who
were long beforehand marked out for this condemnation . . . [who] deny our only Master and Lord, Jesus
Christ.*

JUDE 4

INTRODUCTION

Man is a dependent being. He may think of himself as auton-
omous. He may struggle against authority. He may fly the flag of
independence. But he cannot function without rules. He cannot
live without governance. He cannot survive without God. When
only subjective values remain, when only internal controls are considered valid, when man does that which is right in his own eyes—
then man has died. Only the *animal* remains—the animal and the
law of the jungle.[1]

Certainly no member of the Church could hold to such a philosophy or (can the term be so abused?) theology. Serious Christians
will be tempted to assert that he cannot, and to move on to other
matters. But Jude gives us a short rein.

Why? What does Jude have to say?

JUDE ON "THE SIN OF THE SOUL"

Jude says that there are some in the Church who "deny our only
Master and Lord, Jesus Christ" (v. 4). Perhaps that gives us a
clue as to how they got into the Church. They are not necessarily
atheists or *agnostics* or *skeptics*. They can talk about God and write
theology. It is even possible that they revere Jesus as a good Man, a

	Irreverence	Sensuality	Lawlessness
Designation	Asebeia—ungodliness, impiety, irreverence (v. 4)	Aselgeia—license for immorality, sensuality (v. 4)	Anomia—lawlessness, denying our Lord (v. 4)
Explanations and descriptions	1. "Revile angelic majesties" (v. 8) 2. "Revile [speak abusively]" (v. 10) 3. "Ungodly deeds which they have done" (v. 15) 4. "Grumblers, finding fault" (v. 16) 5. "Mockers" (v. 18)	1. "By dreaming, defile the flesh" (v. 8) 2. Destroyed by "things ... they know by instinct" (v. 10) 3. "Following after their own lusts" 4. "Flattering ... for advantage" (v. 16) 5. "Worldly-minded" (v. 19)	1. They "reject authority" (v. 8) 2. They boast about themselves (v. 16) 3. They "cause divisions" (v. 19)
Metaphors and analogies	1. "Hidden reefs in your love feasts" (v. 12)	1. "Caring for [only] themselves" (v. 12) 2. "Clouds without water, carried along by winds" (v. 12) 3. "Autumn trees without fruit ... uprooted" (v. 12) 4. "Wild waves of the sea" (v. 13)	1. "Wild waves of the sea" (v. 13) 2. "Wandering stars" (v. 13)
Precursors and examples	1. The people of the Exodus (v. 5) 2. Michael the archangel (v. 9) 3. The way of Cain (v. 11)	1. Sodom and Gomorrah (v. 7) 2. Balaam's error (v. 11)	1. The Israelites of the Exodus (v. 5) 2. The angels who did not keep their first rule (v. 6) 3. The rebellion of Korah (v. 11)

great Teacher, and an unparalleled Example. But never in a million years should they have been allowed into the membership of a church. The god to whom they give allegiance is not the God and Father of our Lord Jesus Christ. If they have written any theologies, their theologies are not *Christian* theologies. If they have pointed men to Jesus, they have not pointed them to the Christ of sacred Scripture.

The reason for that conclusion is clear. Those people deny that Jesus is Master (*despotēs*) and Lord (*kyrios*). And, as a matter of fact, the affirmation that He is Master and Lord is at the heart of the Christian faith: "God highly exalted Him, and bestowed on Him the name which is above every name, that at the name of Jesus EVERY KNEE SHOULD BOW . . . and that every tongue should confess that Jesus Christ is Lord, to the glory of God the Father," says Paul (Philippians 2:9-10). In addressing Jesus, His disciples called Him Master and Lord. The confession of the early Christian was: "Jesus Christ is Lord."

But not so in the case of the church people Jude writes about. That which true Christians explicitly affirm, they expressly deny. And to deny His lordship is the fundamental sin of the soul—the seat of our thoughts, our emotions, our will, our self-consciousness. To understand the nature of the soul and its sin is to understand why man tends to be so insensitive to the things of the spirit and so alive to the urgings of the body. For there is a sense in which the soul stands between the spirit and the body and determines which one will be nourished. But the soul is more than a policeman directing traffic "inward" to the spirit or "outward" to the body. It is in our souls that we determine who or what will have the mastery in our lives. And that, after all, is man's ultimate human freedom—the freedom to choose one's master or (in self-deception) to deny all masters.

EXPLANATIONS AND DESCRIPTIONS

Jude made some additional statements that further describe those individuals.

- They reject authority (*kuriotēta*) (v. 8). That phrase is most illuminating. It suggests that those imposters reject not only Christ's authority but any authority outside their own. They insist upon "doing their own thing." They are a law to themselves. They are *anomia.*

• They boast about themselves (v. 16). Naturally. They are *self*-made, *self*-fulfilled, *self*-willed men. Are there any such who do not, in one way or other, put themselves on a pedestal?

• They cause division among believers (v. 19). These men are the ones making "separations." The word for separation is *apodiorizō,* "to mark off" or "to limit." In the New Testament the expression is used only by Jude. He charges these heretics with drawing up their own limits, boundaries, distinctions, definitions. They make up the rules and then invite others to "play the game" according to their regulations. That is as we might expect. Such people are seldom satisfied to attract attention. They want—in fact, they need—a following. How unlike the apostle who writes to the schismatics in Corinth: "What then is Apollos? And what is Paul? *Servants* through whom you believed, even as the *Lord* gave opportunity to each one" (1 Corinthians 3:5, italics added).

METAPHORS AND ANALOGIES

At least two of Jude's figures seem to picture these people in their refusal to submit to Christ's authority.

• They are "wild, foaming waves" (v. 13, NIV). Once again this metaphor fits the case in point. Anyone who has been on a boisterous ocean at night will get the picture. Few natural phenomena seem more uncontrollable, more foreboding than "wild, foaming waves."

• They are "wandering stars" (v. 13). The word for wandering is *planētai,* which means to "go astray." Of course this is the language of appearance, similar to our words *sunrise* and *sunset.* Watch the stars on some clear night. The heavenly bodies are all in their places, following patterned paths ordained by the Creator. All at once one of them goes berserk and, leaving a trail of fire, hurtles along its own path until it is extinguished in the blackness of space. Such is the course chosen by these people. And, sadly, such is their end.

PRECURSORS AND EXAMPLES

Finally, Jude gives three examples of persons who denied lordship and lived to regret it:

1. *The unbelieving Israelites of the Exodus* (v. 5). Previously we have seen how the people of Israel irreverently murmured and grumbled against Jehovah God. But, of course, their sin was more extensive than that. In Numbers 13 and 14 we are told that the people were discouraged from entering Canaan because of the majority report of the spies. The Israelites said, "Let us appoint a leader and return to Egypt" (Numbers 14:4). When Joshua and Caleb heard that they tore their garments and said, "If the Lord is pleased with us, then He will bring us into this land, and give it to us—a land which flows with milk and honey. *Only do not rebel against the* LORD" (Numbers 14:8-9, italics added).

In response, the people were ready to stone Joshua and Caleb. No wonder the Lord asked Moses, "How long will this people spurn Me? And how long will they not believe in Me?" (Numbers 14:11). Clearly the people of Israel were denying the rule of Jehovah. Why should He put up with them? No wonder an entire unbelieving generation died in the barren desert without ever seeing Canaan.

2. *The angels who did not keep their own domain* (*archē*) (v. 6). What possible excuse could be found for the fallen angels? It is true that we do not know the exact circumstances surrounding their defection, though Isaiah 14:12-15 may furnish some clues. Nevertheless, when we realize that from their creation they enjoyed all the goodness of divine rule and all the excellencies of their heavenly calling, it becomes almost incomprehensible that they would follow Lucifer in his rebellion against God. But so it was. And Jude's reference to them is an indication of the seriousness with which he viewed the defection of some churchmen in his day.

3. *The rebellion of Korah* (v. 11). That history was common knowledge among the people to whom Jude was writing. It is recorded in Numbers 16:1-40. Korah, Dathan, and Abiram were envious of Moses and Aaron. They rounded up some 250 followers and challenged God's appointed leaders. But they did it in the manner of deceptive diplomacy. Confronting their leaders they said,

"You have gone far enough, for all the congregation are holy, every one of them, and the LORD is in their midst; so why do you exalt yourselves above the assembly of the LORD?" (Numbers 16:3). Jude calls their speech *antilogia* (back talk). It could not go unchallenged by Moses. Nor could it go unanswered by God. Korah, Dathan, and Abiram and their families were swallowed up in a giant fissure in the earth. Their followers were consumed by fire. And the bronze censers in which they brought incense to the Lord were hammered into plating for the altar—an abiding reminder to Israel that none should usurp the authority of the Lord or the authority of those appointed by Him to rule His people.

THE DENIAL OF GOD IN THE MODERN WORLD

THE BASIC PHILOSOPHY OF MODERN MAN

It is not easy to determine the extent to which the process has been a conscious one, but man—especially Western man—has pushed God farther and farther from himself and the world in modern times. We have seen in the previous chapter how God and His revelation are rendered irrelevant when truth is confined to knowledge that comes through the senses. Nietzsche concluded that man had killed God and that—horrendous thought—it only remained to wipe His blood from the knife! Of course, he was wrong. God has remained very much alive. But all the slogans in the world ("My God is alive. Sorry about yours.") cannot change the fact that, as far as modern man is concerned, natural law governs a good part of the universe, and man himself governs the rest. If modern man does not quite deny the existence of God, he nevertheless denies His rule over nature and, especially, human affairs. And he does this on both community and individual levels. In the depths of his soul the worldling believes that to the extent that natural law does not lord it over man—to the degree to which man is "free"—he is free to make his own rules. William Ernest Henley said it well in his "Invictus":

> I am the master of my fate;
> I am the captain of my soul.[2]

Modern man, therefore, is left with two alternative philosophies.

Either the world is to be regarded as a machine with man as a part of it, or (for some inexplicable reason) man stands outside the machine and has the freedom to assert his own laws (meaning, rules, values, etc.). The first alternative can be termed naturalism or materialism. The second can be called humanism or, better, egotheism.[3] Looking at it from a psychological perspective, Paul Vitz calls it the "cult of self-worship."[4]

EXPRESSIONS AND RESULTS OF MODERN PHILOSOPHY

Francis Schaeffer has devoted considerable effort to an explanation of how the "upper story" (God and supernature) has been disregarded by "modern, modern man." And he has also shown the results of that disregard in philosophy, science, and the arts. Consider but a few examples:

1. *Philosophy*. Having dismissed God from the universe, Nietzsche insisted that in order to "know life" man must ignore all beliefs and conventions. That is a prerequisite to becoming "Overman" or "Superman."

2. *Psychology*. Richard Speck's psychologist argued that Speck could no more keep from killing those (eight Chicago) nurses than another man could keep from sneezing.[5]

3. *Literature*. Albert Camus pictures one of his characters as being human because he overcomes fate by scorn; he labors though labor has no meaning; he rolls a rock up the hill knowing full well that it will roll down again.

4. *Art*. Few artistic productions are more representative of our man-centered era than are the sculptures and sketches of Gustav Vigeland in the famous park and museum in Oslo, which display his works. At the very center of the beautiful park is a monolith containing thirty-six granite groups showing the phases of human life. Of the monolith Vigeland said, "The Monolith is my religion, and it is up to each individual spectator to try to interpret it."[6] It is difficult to see how any interpretation can go beyond man himself— man working out his own destiny.

5. *Music*. John Cage composes music without attention to laws of harmony and rhythm. Notes and rhythm are established by pure

chance in much the same way a gambler rolls the dice. No wonder the members of the New York Philharmonic Orchestra hissed Cage after playing his music.[7]

6. *Language.* Gertrude Stein uses language without attention to the normal rules and syntax and grammar. A typical Stein composition goes like this:

> As I say commas are servile and they have no life of their own, and their use is not a use, it is a way of replacing one's own interest and I do decidedly like to like my own interest my own interest [sic] in what I am doing. A comma by helping you along holding your coat for you and putting on your shoes keeps you from living your life as actively as you should lead it and to me for many years and I still do feel that way about it only now I do not pay as much attention to them, the use of them was positively degrading. Let me tell you what I feel and what I mean and what I felt and what I meant.[8]

The above is just a small sampling of modern man's productions and a not-too-subtle indication of his plight. Modern man wants meaning. "We live," wrote Antoine De Saint-Exupery, "not on things, but on the meaning of things."[9] Modern man also wants freedom, justice, and hope. But without God there is none of those. Without God man is dust with no destiny.

Why does man refuse God? Because he does not want God's *rule.* Denials of God stem from moral rather than intellectual disaffection. That is made abundantly clear in Romans 1:18-25, a passage that gives amazing insight into the psychological dimensions of man's rebellion. Building on its teaching, R. C. Sproul points out that the "psychology of rebellion" consists of three stages: trauma, repression, and substitution. In his quest for personal autonomy, man is threatened by God's self-revelation. Consequently, he represses, or "puts down," this knowledge of God. That which provokes anxiety and personal discomfort is buried in the realm of the subconscious. But it is not destroyed. Instead, this knowledge manifests itself outwardly in a disguised form, that of man-made religion. In legitimizing only that which he himself accepts, man ends up worshiping himself and his own fleshly desires.[10]

That is the spirit of lawless rebellion at work. Of course, it does not change the fact that Christ is Lord. But it changes man. First, it places a question mark after every truth that gives coherence and direction to human life. Anxiety over life's meaning is so pervasive in our society that our age might be appropriately labeled "the age of anxiety." Second, it culminates in the dishonoring of that which is fundamentally human. In the words of Karl Barth, "When God has been deprived of His glory, men are also deprived of theirs. Desecrated within their souls, they are desecrated also without in their bodies, for men are one."[11]

LAWLESSNESS IN THE CHURCH

OVERT AND BLATANT LAWLESSNESS IN THE CHURCH

There are two basic denials in theology that lead to lawlessness. One denial is the denial of the "true God of the Bible." The other is the denial of the "Bible of the true God." Those denials result in a lack of absolutes and ultimately in antinomianism. Let us examine them more closely.

1. *The denial of the God of the Bible.* In past generations that denial took the form of a rejection of the biblical descriptions of God as a God of vengeance and judgment and the acceptance of teachings that depicted God as a loving and beneficent Father. In some of the more modern theologies such as those of Paul Tillich, John A. T. Robinson, Thomas J. J. Altizer, and William Hamilton, however, we have a denial that is more sophisticated and, in some ways, even more fateful.

It is important that we understand the late Paul Tillich. He insisted that the word *God* is a symbol for "ultimate concern." It follows that atheism is not the denial of the God of the Bible (or *any* personal "god"). Atheism is unconcerned about the meaning of one's existence: "He who denies God as a matter of ultimate concern affirms god, because he affirms ultimacy in his concern. God is the fundamental concern for what concerns us ultimately."[12] It follows that, if someone asks whether we should believe in Christ or Mohammed, he has asked the wrong question. "The question of faith is not Moses or Jesus or Mohammed; the question is: Who expresses most adequately one's ultimate concern?"[13]

It is the Anglican bishop John A. T. Robinson who has popularized that point of view. In his book *Honest to God* he says that Feuerbach and Nietzsche were not atheists but "antitheists." They saw "a supreme Person in heaven as the great enemy of man's coming of age. That was the God they must 'kill' if man was not to continue dispossessed and kept in strings."[14] With Tillich, Robinson is convinced that to revolt against such a highest Person is correct. He writes: "It is urgent that we should work away at framing a conception of God and the Christian Gospel which does not depend upon that projection."[15]

That should be sufficient to enable us to understand the "death of God" theology of men like Altizer. It is not the death of the idea of God or talk about God or knowledge about God ("theology") but the death of a transcendent, personal God—and especially the God of the Bible—that is being advocated. Perhaps we should use the past tense here because the death of God theology seems to have gone out of fashion as rapidly as it became fashionable. But has it really? Or does it live on in less recognizable forms?

2. *The denial of the "Bible of God."* Drawing upon Friedrich Schleiermacher, Albert Ritschl, Georg Wilhelm Hegel, and others, classical liberalism put its trust in higher criticism and denied the historic doctrines of revelation and inspiration. It is usually thought to have ended with Karl Barth and his revived interest in, and dependence upon, the Scriptures. To be sure, Barth's neo-orthodoxy did result in a greater appreciation for the Bible even on the part of some liberals. But some liberals still hold that God reveals Himself in all sacred books—the Koran and Bhagavad Gita as well as the Bible—and that the difference between them is one of degree rather than one of kind. Still other liberals give special allegiance to the Bible but believe it to be something less than fully authoritative. G. Bromley Oxnam, for example, acknowledges the revelational aspect of Scripture but insists that human limitations make it something less than completely trustworthy. He writes:

The revelation was conditioned by their [human beings'] ability to understand, and their reports of the limitations that current events, current thought, and current practice evoke. Take the cosmology of the Old Testament writers, for instance; or the belief in demons; or Paul's attitude toward women. To hold that Paul's advice on women is truth revealed by God and binding upon all is as sorry as to hold that God commanded the Jews to commit atrocities on their enemies in war. *Nonetheless, truth is revealed.* [Italics added][16]

This latter approach can rightly be called neo-liberal. It says in effect that divine truth is revealed in the Bible, but man has progressed to the point where he is free to (obligated to?) judge the Bible for himself and decide what he will accept and what he will reject. Moreover, he is no longer obligated to measure other religious claims and spiritual experiences by a biblical standard.

Consider the case of John Dilly, pastor of the First Presbyterian Church of Fairfield, Iowa, as an example of the implications of this denial of biblical authority. Since the followers of Maharishi Maheshi Yogi and his Transcendental Meditation took over a college in Fairfield, Dilly has come to commend T. M. rather than expose it in the light of Scripture. He claims that it is an "effortless" and "natural" way to clear the mind so that the spirit can move more easily toward God. Despite the obvious religious significance of his family's initiation into T.M.—the flowers, the handkerchiefs, the incense burned before "His Divinity, Swami Guru Dev," and the repetition of the mantra—Dilly claims that involvement in T.M. has not compromised his faith in Christ. In fact, he insists that it has made his entire life-style *more* Christian. "I do not pretend to know exactly how and why it works," he says, "but I can attest to the fact that I have never felt so great in my twenty years in the ministry."[17]

3. *The loss of authority in the Church.* It does not require a great deal of thought to see that, however accomplished, the denial of a personal and righteous God and of an objective and authoritative Bible results in a loss of absolutes and leads to *anomia;* Fëdor Mikhailovich Dostoevski was correct when he concluded that if God is dead "everything is allowable."

Of course, in the Church it is not put quite so bluntly. It is given a Christian "twist." Take, for example, Joseph Fletcher's "situation ethics," in which nothing is prescribed except love.[18] Or, consider John A. T. Robinson, who writes: "Nothing can *of itself always* be labeled as 'wrong' (italics added).[19] Still another example is Letty Russell. Our mission, she says, is to make "the world a place where men may find true human community and freedom."[20] With that "mission" in view she says:

> If the world that it serves is secular, then the men also who labor with Christ in that world should be secular, insisting that men live honestly in their own time and history and seeking to fight against any new ideologies that try to force men to live and think in a closed world. Secular Christians are free men—free to smoke, drink, dance, and free not to smoke, drink, dance; free to wear a gray flannel suit, or free to wear a beard; free to read *The Saturday Evening Post, Esquire, Playboy;* free to be snobbish intellectuals; free to be antichurch civil rights workers—in short they are free to be themselves as part of the world in which they live subject only to consideration for their neighbors and for the job that Christ has called them to do (1 Cor. 10:23-24).[21]

In one sense, of course, the approaches of Fletcher, Robinson, and Russell cannot be called lawless because they affirm the law of love. And was it not Jesus Himself who said that all the commandments can be summed up in the great commandment: "YOU SHALL LOVE THE LORD YOUR GOD WITH ALL YOUR HEART, AND WITH ALL YOUR SOUL, AND WITH ALL YOUR MIND," and "YOU SHALL LOVE YOUR NEIGHBOR AS YOURSELF" (Matthew 22:37-39)? And did not Augustine say something to the effect that we should love God and do as we please?

Assuredly so. But that does not end the matter. The love that Jesus and Augustine were talking about was not just *any* love but, first and foremost, love for God. And not just love for any god but, rather, love for the God of the Bible. It is no accident that references to the first commandment in Fletcher's *Situation Ethics* are virtually nonexistent.

Furthermore, the love Jesus and Augustine were talking about was not a love that could be expressed in *any* way, but, first and foremost, it was to be expressed in obedience to the commandments of the divine Scriptures. Jesus said, "If you love me, you will keep my commandments" (John 14:15).

Lawlessness, after all, is not the absence of any and all laws. That would be manifestly impossible. Rather, it is the denial of the right of anyone else "out there"—or even "up there"—to "lord it over" one's life. It is the disregard of any law except that law which is acceptable to one's *self*.

COVERT AND INCIPIENT LAWLESSNESS IN THE CHURCH

There are expressions—or, at least, reflections—of lawlessness in the Church that are not nearly so clear-cut. Only the Lord knows how many such are present. We shall focus on two of them of which all of us may be guilty to some extent.

1. *The refashioned "Father in heaven."* Once they understand what is being said, most Christians are repelled by the suggestion that God is "not there" or that He is dead. He is alive and well—we would stake our lives on it. So, by majority rule, that should end the matter.

But it does not. There is always the possibility that we will fall down before some golden calf thinking it to be the Lamb of God. There is always the possibility that we will refashion God into a Being of our liking. C. S. Lewis says we do not so much want a *father* in heaven as a *grandfather* in heaven.[22] What does he mean?

Our memory goes back to a gathering of three generations of a certain family. The third generation had only one representative—a tow-headed boy of four or five, whose eyes fairly danced with exuberance and not a little impishness. Obviously enjoying his front and center role, he accomplished one eye-catching feat after another. Finally, running out of ideas for exceptional acceptable behavior, he did something bad. Whereupon he stopped short, surveyed his audience, and—avoiding the gaze of his father—made a beeline for his grandfather.

That is why we want a "grandfather in heaven." It is because the Lord "DISCIPLINES" those He loves, "AND He SCOURGES EVERY

SON WHOM He RECEIVES" (Hebrews 12:6). A grandfather may "spoil" his grandson, but no true father will knowingly spoil his own son.

What has happened to discipline in the churches? Candidly and to our shame we must answer that in many churches it has all but disappeared. And how did that come about? Have we, too, removed God from His heaven? No, He is still there. But somehow we have refashioned Him into the image of an aging, benign, always smiling grandfather. Were we to pray truthfully in accordance with our perceptions we would unitedly pray, "Our Grandfather who art in heaven. . . ."

Listen to the author of Hebrews: "If you are without discipline, . . then you are illegitimate children and not sons. . . . We had earthly fathers to discipline us, and we respected them; shall we not much rather be subject to the Father of Spirits, and live?" (Hebrews 12: 8-9).

2. *The reinterpreted freedom on earth.* On every side in the Church we hear protests against legalism, against a Christianity that primarily consists of a variety of dos and don'ts. The protest has a certain validity. Paul himself spoke to the futility of confusing adherence to rules with true religion:

> Since you died with Christ to the basic principles of this world, why, as though you still belonged to it, do you submit to its rules: "Do not handle! Do not taste! Do not touch!"? These are all destined to perish with use, because they are based on human commands and teachings. Such regulations indeed have an appearance of wisdom, with their self-imposed worship, their false humility and their harsh treatment of the body, but they lack any value in restraining sensual indulgence. [Colossians 2:20-23, NIV]

As a matter of fact, Paul has rightly been called the "apostle of liberty." "Am I not free? Am I not an apostle?" (1 Corinthians 9:1), and, "All things are lawful for me" (1 Corinthians 6:12), he wrote to the Corinthians. "Keep standing firm and do not be subject again to a yoke of slavery," he exhorted the Galatians (Galatians 5:1).

But it is imperative that we correctly understand Paul's statements about Christian freedom. Obviously Christian freedom was a problem in his day. Antinomianism had its advocates outside and inside the churches. Some translators believe that Paul was actually quoting those antinomians when he wrote, "All things are lawful for me" (twice) and, "Food is for the stomach, and the stomach is for food," in 1 Corinthians 6:12-13. (See the *New International Version,* where those phrases are set off in quotation marks.) At any rate, evidently there were some in the churches who believed themselves to be released from the ties of "normal" morality because they were liberated from the rule of death and evil powers and translated into the new state of the kingdom of Christ. Since they lived in that new, enlightened "spiritual" state, they were, they thought, not bound by the rules of society that governed the conduct of unbelievers.[23]

That misinterpretation is not limited to the Corinthian church of Paul's day. There are those today who maintain that grace gives freedom in relation to every activity and shatters any classification of acts as intrinsically good or evil.[24] The Campus Christians argue that since Christ broke the Commandments, we are free to do so also. And the Association for the Advancement of Christian Studies (Toronto) argues that the Commandments were historically conditioned and therefore do not apply to us.[25]

A different but similarly misleading logic is to be found in a recent book on homosexuals and homosexuality. The authors argue that to tell homosexuals on the basis of 1 Corinthians 6:9-11 that they must cease expressing their homosexuality before they can be part of God's kingdom is to place them under law rather than under grace. They then say that after conversion "homosexuals must certainly learn to cease from unloving abuses of sexuality," but they leave the question of what those unloving abuses may be to be decided on the basis of behavioral scientists and the testimony of homosexuals. That on the ground that the biblical writers did not know about the "homosexual condition."[26]

There are serious problems with that approach, not the least of which is that it creates confusion. It is true that one who understands the doctrine of salvation by grace will not tell a homosexual to desist from homosexual behavior *in order to be saved.* One does not earn salvation by doing good deeds or by refraining from evil deeds. But all persons, including homosexuals, need to know that the God of grace is still a God of righteousness, who judges men by His revealed standards. Further, they need to know that only by repenting of deviations from that standard and coming to Christ can they be saved and obtain the power to walk in newness of life. In a word, law must be understood before grace can be appreciated or appropriated. The discipline of grace is not a divine surprise that He springs willy-nilly on the new Christian.

Paul was not saying, "Do this and don't do that and you will be saved." But neither was he saying, "Don't be concerned about your behavior until you are saved." Rightly interpreted, Paul did not make the sounds of a legalist. Neither did he sound like a libertine.

Before bringing this discussion to a close, it may be helpful to look briefly at some principles that are all-important in walking the tightrope between legalism and license.

First, it should be clear that adherence to rules does not necessarily involve one in legalism. For example, a Christian institution may legislate certain activities such as a dormitory curfew, in order to preserve order. Nor does freedom from rules necessarily indicate that one is living "in grace," as Paul makes clear when he talks about not being enslaved by any practice (1 Corinthians 6:12). When it comes to power and motivation for Christian living, grace and law are antithetical. But there can be grace in law, just as there can be law in grace.[27]

Second, the Christian is not obligated to keep the law *as a means of salvation,* nor must he constantly perform good works or refrain from certain "social evils" in *a ceaseless quest to gain God's approval.* Our position before God is one of acceptance through Christ (Galatians 5:1).

Third, Christian liberty has as its highest goal and motivation the glory of God (1 Corinthians 10:31; Colossians 3:17). The Christian exchanges involuntary servitude to self for voluntary servitude to Christ. If a Christian cannot honestly ask for God's blessing on a certain activity, then it is wrong. Thus, Christian service is guided by the law. Adultery is never an option for a believer. Yet, this service is performed, not as an external conformity to the demands of the law, but as an internal response to the pull of grace. That is what it means to be under the "law of grace" (Romans 6).

Fourth, the Christian should do nothing that would violate his conscience or hinder fellowship with God (1 Timothy 1:5). That is to imply that there is a need for both personal discipline and freedom. Both are necessary aspects of responsibility, as Christ often made clear. His words in the Sermon on the Mount reveal that fulfillment of the requirements of internal purity are more demanding and require more discipline than mere external conformity to law, human or divine. At the same time, His controversy with the Pharisees reveals the impropriety and danger of setting up an exhaustive list of rules that would govern what every individual should do in every situation. In matters not specifically dealt with in Scripture, what may defile the conscience or be a temptation for one person may be perfectly harmless for another. Currently there are two tendencies that threaten to stifle true spirituality in evangelical churches. One is a sorry lack of personal discipline, and the other is an emphasis upon external regulation and control.

Fifth, Christian liberty must be exercised with the well-being of other believers in mind. True love will always lead us to relinquish that to which we may be legitimately entitled for the sake of another (1 Corinthians 6:12; 8:9; Galatians 5:13). Stated negatively, this principle means that we should avoid activities that will hinder the spiritual growth of another believer. Stated positively, it means that we should do everything possible to help a Christian brother or sister in need. In a culture dominated by individualism and the philosophy of "personal rights," Christians find it particularly hard to put that principle into practice. But what a difference self-sacrifice for the sake of others could make in the Church!

Finally, Christian liberty must never be exercised in such a way that it hinders our testimony to unbelievers (1 Corinthians 10:32-33; 1 Peter 3:11). Carl F. H. Henry puts it well: "The Christian's walk must not give the lie to his confession. It is rather to buttress the witness of his mouth."[28]

CONCLUSION

Admittedly, Jude comes down hard on those who are guilty of lawlessness. The fact that they have found a way into the Church helps them not a whit. If they deny Jesus Christ, who is Sovereign and Lord, all else is pretense.

There is a passage in 1 John 3 that is remarkable both for the questions it has occasioned and for the clarity it brings to our present concern. The questions cluster around the translation of verse 9 in the King James Version: "Whosoever is born of God doth not commit sin; for his seed remaineth in him: and he cannot sin, because he is born of God." The questions arise because it is obvious that we all sin in thought, word, and deed. None is perfect. What, then, does John mean? The problem is resolved—at least in part—by such translations as the *New International Version,* which keeps the continuous action of the Greek verb: "No one who is born of God will continue to sin." We say "in part" because, though Christians grow in obedience, they do "continue in sin" even though they do not "sin continually." "If we say that we have no sin, we are deceiving ourselves" (1 John 1:8).

We believe that the passage should be interpreted in the light of the *kind* of sin with which John is concerned. Notice 1 John 3:4: "Everyone who practices sin also practices lawlessness; and sin is lawlessness." Ultimately, that is what sin is—lawlessness. And that must be taken into account. It is one thing to sin and confess that sin and be forgiven (1 John 1:9). It is another thing to sin and contend that no one, including the Christ of God, has a right to issue commands to us, a right to rule our lives. The first is disobedience. The latter is lawlessness. Christians may disobey at times. But they will never be lawless.

Jesus Christ *is* Sovereign and Lord.

NOTES

1. For a complete discussion see C. S. Lewis, *The Abolition of Man* (New York: Macmillan, 1947).

2. William Ernest Henley, "Invictus," in John Ciardi, ed., *How Does a Poem Mean?* (Boston: Houghton Mifflin, 1959), p. 848.

3. Robert Brow, *Religion: Origins and Ideas* (Chicago: Inter-Varisty, 1966).

4. Paul Vitz, *Psychology as Religion: The Cult of Self-Worship* (Grand Rapids: Eerdmans, 1977).

5. Francis Schaeffer, *Death in the City* (Downers Grove, Ill.: Inter-Varsity, 1969), p. 104.

6. Quoted in a travel folder prepared by a Norwegian government agency.

7. Francis Schaeffer, *The Church at the End of the Twentieth Century* (Downers Grove, Ill.: Inter-Varsity, 1970), pp. 21-22.

8. Gertrude Stein, "Parts, Speech and Punctuation" in *The Limits of Language,* ed. Walker Gibson (New York: Hill and Wang, 1962), pp. 87-88.

9. Cited by Paul Tournier, *The Meaning of Persons* (New York: Harper & Row, 1957), p. 186.

10. R. C. Sproul, *The Psychology of Atheism* (Minneapolis: Bethany Fellowship, 1974), pp. 73-80.

11. Ibid., p. 69.

12. Paul Tillich, *Dynamics of Faith* (New York: Harper & Row, 1958), p. 46.

13. Ibid., p. 66.

14. John A. T. Robinson, *Honest to God* (Philadelphia: Westminster, 1963), p. 41.

15. Ibid., p. 43.

16. Bromley G. Oxnam, *A Testament of Faith* (Boston: Little, 1958), p. 135.

17. "T.M. Comes to the Heartland of the Midwest," *Christian Century,* 10 December 1975, pp. 1129-1131.

18. Joseph Fletcher, "A New Look in Christian Ethics," *Harvard Divinity Bulletin* (October 1959), pp. 7-18.

19. Robinson, p. 118.

20. Letty M. Russell, *Christian Education in Mission* (Philadelphia: Westminster, 1967), p. 130.

21. Ibid.

22. C. S. Lewis, *The Problem of Pain* (New York: Macmillan, 1978), p. 28.

23. John W. Drane, *Paul, Libertine or Legalist?* (London: S.P.C.K., 1975), pp. 101-5.

24. Jacques Ellul, *The Ethics of Freedom* (Grand Rapids: Eerdmans, 1976), pp. 187-210.

25. Gordon Clark, *1 Corinthians: A Contemporary Commentary* (Nutley, N.J.: Presbyterian and Reformed, 1975).

26. Letha Scanzoni and Virginia Ramey Mollenkott, *Is the Homosexual My Neighbor?* (New York: Harper & Row, 1978), pp. 69-71.

27. Charles C. Ryrie, *Balancing the Christian Life* (Chicago: Moody, 1969), pp. 151-62.

28. Carl F. H. Henry, *Christian Personal Ethics* (Grand Rapids: Eerdmans, 1959), p. 433.

QUESTIONS FOR REFLECTION AND DISCUSSION

1. Reflect on the following question: "Do I truly believe in the God revealed in Scripture, or do I tend to distort Him in order to suit my own inclination?

2. While the world says that there can be no freedom without complete autonomy, Scripture states that autonomy from God results

only in bondage, whereas slavery to God makes man truly free. How do the apostle Paul's life and testimony demonstrate the scriptural position (cf. Romans 6:15-23)?

3. John Stott has remarked: "I am suggesting, therefore, that it is as unbiblical as it is unrealistic to divorce the Lordship from the Saviorhood of Jesus Christ." And Arthur Kirk states, in even stronger language: "Those preachers who tell sinners that they may be saved without surrendering to the Lordship of Christ are as erroneous and dangerous as others who insist that salvation is by works" (cited in Charles C. Ryrie, *Balancing the Christian Life,* p. 169). Do you agree or disagree? Can one be saved without submitting to Christ as Lord? (See Acts 2:36; Romans 10:9; 1 Corinthians 12:3.) What does it mean to acknowledge Christ as "Lord"? (See John 20:28; Acts 2:36; 10:36; Jude 4-5.)

4. How would you define the following words: "liberty," "license," and "legalism"? In what sense can we say that there is grace in the law? Law in grace? How might both license and legalism be exercised as part of the "cult of self-worship"?

5. To what extent is Romans 1:18-32 an accurate picture of our society? Do you agree with Sproul's description of the "psychology of rebellion"?

Part Three

PROPHECY

7

THE PROPHECY OF APOSTASY AND THE END OF THE AGE

Enoch, in the seventh generation from Adam, proph-
esied . . . "Behold, the Lord came . . . to execute judg-
ment. . . . But you, beloved, ought to remember the words
that were spoken beforehand by the apostles of our Lord
Jesus Christ, that they were saying to you, "In the last
time . . ."

JUDE 14-15, 17-18

General: The nature of prophecy	The "double vision" of the prophets
Specific: The "last times"	The "age of the end"—the church age The "end of the age"—the final act of history
Parables: The "prophetic alert"	The householder surprised by a thief The wise servant and the wicked servant The wise virgins and the foolish virgins

INTRODUCTION

The Scriptures speak of widespread apostasy as being one of the earmarks of the period immediately preceding Christ's return. Apostasy is nothing new. There have been cases of "falling away" from the faith throughout the history of the Church. The apostasy

85

of the final days, however, will be qualitatively different from, and more terrible than, anything previously experienced. Paul calls it "the apostasy" of the end times (2 Thessalonians 2:3). The visible Church will forsake the true faith and in the process become the vehicle of Satan-inspired and Satan-energized religion. Indeed, one of the most amazing aspects of biblical prophecy is its revelation that in the end times the occult will merge with false religion, engulfing even many who call themselves Christians.

The picture is a grim one. Spirits will be loosed from the "abyss," or "prison of the demons" (Revelation 9:1-12), signaling an unparalleled outburst of Satanic activity (Revelation 9:20) and the rise of the Antichrist, his false prophet, and the harlot church (Revelation 13:1-18; 17). Armed with the power of Satan, the Antichrist and his followers will seek to accredit themselves through extravagant displays of power, supernatural signs, and deceiving wonders (2 Thessalonians 2:9). Religious leaders will freely use the names of God and His Christ and employ religious terminology, but only to conceal the ultimate demonic origin of their supernatural feats (Matthew 7:21-23; 24:24).[1]

Perceptive believers sense that there is an important connection between what is happening in our day and what will transpire in the future. But what *is* the connection? Can we analyze present developments, feed the resulting information into a "prophetic computer," and arrive at a "reading" as to where present events fit on the divine calendar?

Jude speaks to those concerns. But before we examine his words it will be helpful to look into the nature of biblical prophecy and the teaching of Christ on the subject at hand.

THE NATURE OF BIBLICAL PROPHECY

The prophets of the Old Testament possessed a "double vision" of future events. They were not in need of corrective surgery, however. It was the normal way in which they viewed divine communication concerning future events. Historical events and persons familiar to the prophets were frequently mingled with events and persons of much later times, so that the two appeared to be almost indistinguishable. The fulfillment of the first became a foreshadowing of the fulfillment of the second.

Samuel, for example, predicted an offspring of David whose throne would be established forever (2 Samuel 7:12-16). Obviously, that prophecy was not entirely fulfilled in Solomon (although there are certain elements in the prophecy that could refer only to him). Was Samuel mistaken? No. Rather, the reign of Solomon foreshadowed the final fulfillment in the reign of Christ, as the writer of Hebrews makes clear (Hebrews 1:5).

Take another example. The prophet Joel saw in a locust plague the portent of a future invasion of Israel by Assyria. The two events were separated chronologically, although in Joel's mind they were graphically linked together. Furthermore, Joel presented the coming invasion as a foreshadowing of the final day of the Lord—a new spiritual age, which was inaugurated at Pentecost but which will reach its climax at the time of the second coming (Joel 2:28-32; Acts 2:28-33).

CHRIST'S PROPHECY OF THE END TIMES

We will save ourselves much grief and misunderstanding if we bear in mind that the New Testament writers often thought and expressed themselves in the same way as did the Old Testament prophets. Jesus and the apostles were not bound by twentieth-century thought forms. Being a part of the same cultural milieu as the Old Testament prophets, our Lord and the apostles looked at future events from the "prophetic perspective."

In the Olivet Discourse (Matthew 24; Luke 21) Jesus predicted the presence of certain "signs" of the end times—among them religious chaos and the rise of false prophets. Throughout history, commentators have taken those words to refer to either the events surrounding the fall of Jerusalem in A.D. 70 *or* the events of the Tribulation preceding Christ's return. Both interpretations entail serious problems though both seem to have validity. Which is true? The answer is that both are true.

The initial fulfillment of Jesus' predictions of famines, wars, persecution and false prophets is graphically depicted in Josephus'

Antiquities, where he describes the horrors that accompanied the fall of Jerusalem to the Roman armies. Christ obviously connected those events with the events at the end of world history (Matthew 24:29). He made clear that His coming would be preceded by an indefinite period of time (Matthew 24:36) called the "times of the Gentiles," during which the nation of Israel would suffer humiliation (Luke 21:24). Quite in keeping with the prophetic tradition, Jesus viewed the impending crisis *within* history as a foreshadowing of the final crisis at the *end* of history. Stephen Travis puts it well: "The successive embodiments of antichrist foreshadow the final outburst of the devil's rebellion before the end."[2]

There is one more element of Christ's prediction concerning which there has been much misunderstanding. When the disciples questioned Jesus about the end times, they wanted a foolproof method of determining when the end would occur. In their eagerness to be "relevant," modern interpreters exhibit the same curiosity. Many of them find special significance in Jesus' use of the words "birth pangs" in Matthew 24:8. Jesus, they say, compared the presence of wars, earthquakes, famines, false prophets, and the like to the pains that accompany the birth of a child. The increased number and intensity of those signs signal that the climax is upon us. For example, speaking of the final apostate church, Hal Lindsay writes: "Some of you may be thinking that every generation has seen this apostasy in the church. This is true, but the Bible says that as the countdown before Christ's return comes closer, the teachings of the false leaders of the church will depart farther and farther from God's Word."[3]

There is a problem with that approach. Throughout the history of the Church some Christians have looked upon certain dramatic events as a fulfillment of our Lord's prediction about the "signs" that would precede His return. The extreme to which some have gone illustrates the difficulty—indeed, the impossibility—or correctly "reading" the significance of certain events from our limited vantage point. For example, the enthusiasm of the first Crusades was occasioned in part by the belief of many of the participants that they were actors in the final consummation towards which all of history is moving. Convinced that what they saw around them were the signs that were to mark the beginning of the last days, many marched confidently on Jerusalem armed with the expectation that the Antichrist would be met and defeated, and the millennial Kingdom inaugurated.[4] Our readers are likely aware of the sorry train of events that went to make up that unfortunate chapter of the Church's history.

Currently, the danger of that same kind of mentality is very real. According to *Christianity Today,* certain fundamentalist groups are so confident that what they see are the signs accompanying the end, that they are "stockpiling food, stashing weapons and building forti-fied 'retreat' hideaways in preparation for a last stand against the hordes of evil." Influenced by the appeals of evangelist John Todd, some are reported to have said that they would rather kill their chil-dren than allow their families to be tortured.[5]

More than ever we need clear and sober thinking about what the Scriptures do and do not teach in this regard. The signs of which Christ spoke are *not* the birthpangs themselves but preliminary events only. They point to the events of the end and are a kind of "pledge" that they will take place—but the signs themselves are not part of the final act of history. In fact, nowhere do the Scriptures specifically teach that we can use those signs as a time clock in order to determine where we are in God's program for world history. Rather, they constitute a "prophetic alert"—a reminder that God is faithful and redemption is in the offing.

Furthermore—and this is particularly significant—these events characterize the Church age in its entirety, from the resurrection to the second coming. This entire period of history is called the "latter times" or the "last days," as Peter made clear in his sermon at Pente-cost (Acts 2:14). Of course, as Christianity has grown from its first-century home in the region of the Mediterranean to become the world religion that it is today, apostasy has become more wide-spread. But it is not made qualitatively different in the twentieth century simply by being more widespread. Almost from the begin-ning, apostasy has been a feature of Church history and one of the indications that we live in the "last times."

With the foregoing in mind, look once again at the parabolic warnings Jesus gives in connection with His discussion of the "signs of the times." First, He speaks of the householder whose house was broken into by a thief. If the man of the house had known the time of the break-in beforehand, he would have stayed up and kept watch and prevented it. "So," Jesus says, "you must be ready, because the Son of Man will come at an hour when you do not expect him" (Matthew 24:44, NIV).

Next, Jesus differentiates between the wise, faithful servant and the wicked servant. Both are put in charge of the household and told to care for the other servants while the master is away. The wise servant is found doing just that when the master returns. The wicked servant says to himself, "My master is staying away a long time." He beats the other servants and carouses with drunkards. So, Jesus says, "The master . . . will come on a day when he [the servant] does not expect him and at an hour which he does not know, and shall cut him in pieces" (Matthew 24:50-51).

Finally, Jesus tells the familiar parable of the wise and foolish virgins. The five wise virgins took lamps and some extra oil and went to meet the bridegroom. The five foolish virgins took their lamps but no extra oil. The evening dragged on, and all ten went to sleep. At midnight the bridegroom appeared. The wise trimmed their lamps and joined the bridegroom in the banquet hall. The foolish virgins had to go to buy more oil. By the time they returned, it was too late. Therefore, warns Jesus, "Be on the alert then, for you do not know the day nor the hour" (Matthew 25:13).

Note that there was no way for the householder, the servants, and the virgins to know the time when the thief, master, and bridegroom would come. Nevertheless they should have been prepared. The householder should have had his house and goods secured at all times. The servant should not have assumed that his master would delay his coming. He should have acted responsibly every day. The virgins should not have assumed that the bridegroom would come immediately. They should have taken an extra supply of oil.

We conclude, then, that Jesus' purpose in the Olivet Discourse was not to satisfy His disciples' curiosity about when the end of the age would occur but rather to assure them that He would return in the end times and to encourage faithfulness and vigilance on their part. He was not concerned with, as Travis puts it, giving the disciples a "futurologist's sliderule" by which they could determine exactly when He would come. In fact, He warned of the dangers of jumping to premature conclusions.

> Then he said to his disciples, "The time is coming when you will long to see one of the days of the Son of Man, but you will not see it. Men will tell you, 'There he is!' or 'Here he is!' Do not go running off after them. For the Son of Man in his day will be like the lightning, which flashes and lights up the sky from one end to the other." [Luke 17:22, NIV]

> He replied, "Watch out that you are not deceived. For many will come in my name, claiming, 'I am he,' and, 'The time is near.' Do not follow them. When you hear of wars and revolutions, do not be frightened. These things must happen first, but the end will not come right away." [Luke 21:8-9, NIV]

Nevertheless, the signs point to the fact that, at the time appointed by the Father, He is coming. Do not be caught unawares, like the householder. Do not assume that you have time to get straightened around, like the wicked servant. Do not assume that there is no time for any other concerns, like the foolish virgins. Just be assured that He is coming and be ready.

Conclusion

Now we can understand why Jude regarded the apostates of his day as being a direct and literal fulfillment of predictions that "in the last time there shall be mockers, following after their own ungodly lusts" (v. 18). He was not mistaken either in recognizing the apostasy of his day as the fulfillment of prophecy or in identifying his day with the last days. Nor do we err when we recognize the apostasy of our day as the fulfillment of prophecy and identify *our* day with the last days. Obviously, the final redemption is nearer in the twentieth century than it was in the first. It is nearer than when we ourselves first believed. But exactly how near? Of that we cannot be sure. True believers will neither set a date in the distant future in order to justify sinful indulgence, nor will they set a date in the immediate future in order to counteract spiritual indolence. Whether they belong to the twentieth century or to the first, true believers will always be ready for His coming and the end of the age.

NOTES

1. Merrill Unger, *Beyond the Crystal Ball* (Chicago: Moody, 1973), p. 19.
2. Stephen Travis, *The Jesus Hope* (Downers Grove, Ill.: Inter-Varsity, 1976), p. 41.
3. Hal Lindsey with C. C. Carlson, *The Late Great Planet Earth* (Grand Rapids: Zondervan, 1970), p. 128.
4. Norman Cohn, *The Pursuit of the Millennium* (New York: Oxford U. Press, 1961), pp. 54-55.
5. *Christianity Today,* 2 February 1979, pp. 38-42.

QUESTIONS FOR REFLECTION AND DISCUSSION

1. What practical difference should the expectation of Christ's coming make in our lives? Do you think that Paul's instructions in 1 Corinthians 7:25-35 apply to us as much as to the Corinthian church?
2. To what extent are people in the Church today guilty of the same error as the disciples; namely, searching for a way of determining when the end of the age will occur?
3. What is the significance of the "signs" that Christ speaks of for the Church?
4. Do you agree that the Olivet Discourse reflects a prophetic "double vision"? Which of Christ's predictions do you think apply primarily to the fall of Jerusalem? Which elements refer to the events connected with the second coming? What difficulties do you see with totally applying Christ's predictions to the time of the final Tribulation?
5. What are the practical implications of Christ's parables of the householder, the wicked servant, and the virgins? How can a church avoid the errors illustrated in those parables?

8

THE PROPHECIES OF A PATRIARCH AND THE APOSTLES

And about these also Enoch, in the seventh generation from Adam, prophesied, saying, "Behold, the Lord came with many thousands of His holy ones, to execute judgment upon all, and to convict all the ungodly of all their ungodly deeds which they have done in an ungodly way, and of all the harsh things which ungodly sinners have spoken against Him." . . . But you, beloved, ought to remember the words that were spoken beforehand by the apostles of our Lord Jesus Christ, that they were saying to you, "In the last time there shall be mockers, following after their own ungodly lusts."

JUDE 14-15, 17-18

The Person	The Prophecy
The patriarch Enoch	"The Lord came . . . to convict the ungodly"
The apostles: 1. Peter	"There will . . . be false teachers among you, who will secretly introduce destructive heresies" (2 Peter 2:1)
2. Paul	"In later times some will fall away from the faith, paying attention to deceitful spirits and doctrines of demons" (1 Timothy 4:1)
3. John	"Test the spirits . . . because many false prophets have gone out into the world" (1 John 4:1)

INTRODUCTION

Though we must not speak presumptuously about the time of Christ's coming, we dare not disregard the prophetic significance of what is happening in the world and in the Church. Jude says that we must remember what has been prophesied. In keeping with his counsel, notice that Jude calls attention to the earliest and latest relevant prophecies—that of Enoch and those of the apostles.

ENOCH'S PROPHECY

So that there can be no doubt about which Enoch Jude has in mind, he specifically says that Enoch was the seventh from Adam. From Genesis 5:18-24 we learn that this Enoch fathered Methuselah at the age of 65, that he "walked with God," and that he was translated into the presence of God without seeing death at 365 years of age. It is Jude, not Moses, however, who informs us that Enoch left a prophecy concerning apostates to the effect that "behold, the Lord came with many thousands of His holy ones, to execute judgment upon all, and to convict all the ungodly of all their ungodly deeds which they have done in an ungodly way, and of all the harsh things which ungodly sinners have spoken against Him" (Jude 14-15).

Jude's reference to Enoch's prophecy raises a question as to his source. Was he relying on the apocryphal *Book of Enoch?* Some early church fathers thought so and concluded that that book must be inspired because Jude endorsed it. Some recent scholars have concluded just the opposite: Since Jude quoted and endorsed the *Book of Enoch,* Jude's own book must not be inspired, or he would not have done so.

R. C. H. Lenski points out that the assumptions and conclusions of both groups are erroneous. Jude is quoting Enoch, not some apocryphal book that may or may not be an accurate record of what Enoch prophesied.[1] The *Book of Enoch* and Jude's book say essentially the same thing, but that neither adds to the credibility of the one nor detracts from the credibility of the other.

Whatever Jude's source of information regarding Enoch's prophecy might have been, his reference to it is significant. Why? Because of all the signs connected with Christ's second coming, the presence of false teachers in the last days of the church age is particularly emphasized by the biblical writers. The close relationship between apostasy and the final judgment is one that comes up again and again. In order to more fully understand the nature of that relationship we must take a closer look at the writings of the apostles.

THE APOSTLES' PROPHECIES

In connection with Jude's reference to the prophecies of the apostles, two facts are obvious. First, the teaching of the apostles on apostasy and final judgment must have been common knowledge among the churches even at an early date. Second, their teaching merits a far more detailed treatment than we can afford here. Hundreds—perhaps thousands—of volumes have been written on the subject. Our purpose is merely to point out some of the "apostolic words" Jude likely had in mind.

PETER'S PROPHECIES

> But false prophets also arose among the people, just as there will also be false teachers among you, who will secretly introduce destructive heresies, even denying the Master who bought them, bringing swift destruction upon themselves. And many will follow their sensuality, and because of them the way of truth will be maligned; and in their greed they will exploit you with false words; their judgment from long ago is not idle, and their destruction is not asleep. [2 Peter 2:1-3]

> This is now, beloved, the second letter I am writing to you in which I am stirring up your sincere mind by way of reminder, that you should remember the words spoken beforehand by the holy prophets and commandment of the Lord and Savior spoken by your apostles. Know this first of all, that in the last days mockers will come with their mocking, following after their own lusts, and saying, "Where is the promise of His coming?" [2 Peter 3:1-4a]

The similarity between Jude and Peter at this point is apparent—so much so that many commentators have concluded that Jude was dependent upon Peter's letter in writing his own. Others have concluded that Peter was dependent upon the book of Jude. The former is more likely the case because, according to Jude, the falling away prophesied by Peter had already occurred. It is significant that the word Peter uses for "mockers" and the word Jude uses are the same. It is not at all unlikely that Jude had 2 Peter 3:3 in mind.

Jude's use of the words "spoken beforehand" does not mean, of course, that Jude is separating himself from the apostles in such a way that only he is living in the "last times." We have already pointed out that the other apostles themselves thought they were living in that last chapter of world history (2 Timothy 3:1; Hebrews 1:2; 1 John 2:18). Nevertheless, it is likely that Jude saw the developments of his day as unique and regarded the presence of scoffers as further positive proof that the final period of history, which would culminate in the Lord's return, was indeed in the process of unfolding.

The sceptics spoken of by Peter and Jude pointed to the failure of the expected parousia of Christ to occur as justification for their immoral conduct. "If there is no judgment," they reasoned, "we are free to do as we please." How typical! Not long ago, the outspoken atheist Madalyn Murray O'Hair offered the fact that God has not destroyed her as proof that He does not exist.

The concern of Jude and Peter is to show that God is not powerless to fulfill His promises. But their emphasis is different. Jude shows that God's *justice demands* punishment. It is inevitable. Peter alerts us to the fact that God's *mercy explains* the delay of that judgment. God is patient, "not wishing for any to perish but for all to come to repentance" (2 Peter 3:9). Just where mercy ends and justice begins is something we cannot presume to know. It is a mystery known only to God.

PAUL'S PROPHECIES

Certain Pauline passages and phrases regarding a "falling away" come to mind immediately:

> But the Spirit explicitly says that in later times some will fall away from the faith, paying attention to deceitful spirits and doctrines of demons, by means of the hypocrisy of liars seared in their own

conscience as with a branding iron, men who forbid marriage and advocate abstaining from foods, which God has created to be gratefully shared in by those who believe and know the truth. For everything created by God is good, and nothing is to be rejected, if it is received with gratitude; for it is sanctified by means of the word of God and prayer. In pointing out these things to the brethren, you will be a good servant of Christ Jesus, constantly nourished on the words of the faith and of the sound doctrine which you have been following. [1 Timothy 4:1-6]

But realize this, that in the last days difficult times will come. For men will be lovers of self . . . holding to a form of godliness, although they have denied its power; and avoid such men as these . . . always learning and never able to come to the knowledge of the truth. [2 Timothy 3:1-7]

For the time will come when they will not endure sound doctrine; but wanting to have their ears tickled, they will accumulate for themselves teachers in accordance to their own desires; and will turn away their ears from the truth, and will turn aside to myths. [2 Timothy 4:3-4]

Now we request you, brethren, with regard to the coming of our Lord Jesus Christ, and our gathering together to Him, that you may not be quickly shaken from your composure or be disturbed either by a spirit or a message or a letter as if from us, to the effect that the day of the Lord has come. Let no one in any way deceive you, for it will not come unless the apostasy comes first, and the man of lawlessness is revealed, the son of destruction, who opposes and exalts himself above every so-called god or object of worship, so that he takes his seat in the temple of God, displaying himself as being God. [2 Thessalonians 2:1-4]

Paul clearly teaches that the last days will be characterized by heresy and apostasy. But he provides some "new wrinkles" not found in either Peter or Jude. It appears that Paul is predicting that within the period of the "last times" there would be shorter seasons of stress especially characterized by the activity of false teachers (1 Timothy 4:1-2). In any case he is clearly teaching that "deceiving spirits" will be the agents used by Satan to turn men away from true Christian faith. Coming to a person in times of intellectual doubt, devastating sorrow, spiritual failure, or bodily weakness, they sow the seeds of deception. In some instances that kind of temptation may be patently obvious, as in the case of the late Bishop Pike, who, in a desperate and vain attempt to communicate with his deceased son, renounced the faith to which he had given lip service and became progressively enmeshed in the world of the occult.

Christians should not allow an overreading of such developments to upset their spiritual equilibrium. Paul is careful to make a distinction between the "man of lawlessness" and the "mystery of lawlessness." The former is the final and supreme embodiment of evil, the Antichrist who will lead a final widespread and violent rebellion against God's authority. The stage is being set for that. According to historian Arnold Toynbee: "By making more and more lethal weapons, and at the same time making the world more and more interdependent economically, technology has brought mankind to such a degree of distress that we are ripe for the deifying of any Caesar who might succeed in giving the world unity and peace.[2]

But, at the same time, Paul clearly instructs us not to become unsettled. The spirit of antichrist is always present. That is what Paul means by the "mystery of lawlessness." "Mystery" denotes that which is secret and hidden from men, a secret activity of lawlessness. Although the "man of lawlessness" is yet to be revealed, the spirit underlying his activity is always at work and finds expression in anyone who sets himself up against Christ.

JOHN'S PROPHECIES

Beloved, do not believe every spirit, but test the spirits to see whether they are from God; because many false prophets have gone out into the world. By this you know the Spirit of God: every spirit that confesses that Jesus Christ has come in the flesh is from God; and every spirit that does not confess Jesus is not from God; and this is the spirit of the antichrist, of which you have heard that it is coming, and now it is already in the world. You are from God, little children, and have overcome them; because greater is He who is in you than he who is in the world. They are from the world; therefore they speak as from the world, and the world listens to them. We are from God; he who knows

God listens to us; he who is not from God does not listen to us.
By this we know the spirit of truth and the spirit of error. [1 John
4:1-6]

John is particularly sensitive to the tension that exists between
the world and the Church, between the Spirit of truth and the spirit
of error. Why? Because he places this conflict within the context
of its culmination. "Children, it is the *last* hour" (1 John 2:18, italics added), he writes. Just as the final minutes of a closely fought
football game are characterized by special intensity, so, for John, the
fact that the end is "near" makes the spiritual conflict that much
more acute.

But, once again, we must ask ourselves, In what sense did John
think it was the "last hour"? Some have interpreted him to mean
that he thought he was witnessing the beginnings of the great revolt
that would culminate in the return of Christ in his generation. In
addition to the fact that this would make John the author of error,
such an interpretation runs into two other difficulties. First, it fails
to harmonize with Paul's specific instructions that Christians were
not to be unduly alarmed by the presence of many antichrists. Their
presence does not indicate that the "day of the Lord" has arrived
(2 Thessalonians 2:1-4). Second, given Christ's words about the
unpredictability of the "day and the hour" of His return (Mark
13:32) it is unlikely that the apostle John would presume to fore-
cast it in this manner.

Is there any other way in which we can legitimately understand
John's words? Assuredly so. Turn again to the illustration of the
football game. Suppose that the players themselves have no idea of
its duration: the whistle signaling the end of the game could be
blown *at any time*. In that case, from the vantage point of the time-
keeper the game may not, at a particular point, be near its close. But
from the perspective of the players the end is always imminent. For
them the significance of time changes dramatically. No longer is
each passing minute thought of as being simply another minute in a
long series leading to the end of the game; each minute is very much
a part of that end. It is charged with excitement. *It could be the last
minute!* This, we believe, is what John means in stating that it is the

"last hour." He is thinking in terms of the quality of time, not so much of duration. As John Newman has so aptly put it, time runs "not towards the end but along it, and on the brink of it; and it is at all times near that great event. . . . Christ, then, is ever at our doors."[3]

In that sense the Church must always identify itself with the final countdown. The line that separates the events of time from the events of eternity is, in a very real sense, razor thin. It can be crossed at any time. For that reason it is all the more important that we know what we believe and why. Test the spirits, warns John. Be able to distinguish the real from the counterfeit. Your life depends upon it.

Conclusion

Jude by no means stands alone in his insistence that spiritual reversions will be common throughout the entire period of history known as "the last days" or "the last times." His primary purpose in calling forth prophetic witnesses to that fact is not to prove to his readers that the last days are upon us, though that is the case. Rather, he wants to make sure that we are neither discouraged by the presence of apostasy nor deceived by its preachments.

Discouragement, after all, is a real danger. It is relatively easy to hold the Christian banner high and march faithfully forward when surrounded by an army of believing, disciplined Christian soldiers. But when the orders are confused, when division enters the ranks, when the soldiers start marching in diverse directions—then one is tempted to say, "What's the use?" or, "Why buck the tide?"

And when we are discouraged, even a little, we somehow lose our powers of discrimination. Wrong dons the clothing of right. Error masquerades as truth. And we may be deceived.

Jude—and Enoch, and Paul, and Peter, and John, and our Lord Himself—prophesy in order to spare us such a plight.

NOTES

1. R. C. H. Lenski, *The Interpretation of the Epistles of St. Peter, St. John and St. Jude* (Minneapolis: Augsburg, 1966), pp. 641-42.

2. Cited in Stephen Travis, *The Jesus Hope* (Downers Grove, Ill.: Inter-Varsity, 1974), p. 44.
3. Cited in F. F. Bruce, *The Epistles of John* (Grand Rapids: Eerdmans, 1979), p. 65.

QUESTIONS FOR REFLECTION AND DISCUSSION

1. What is the significance of the apostles' teachings about apostasy for understanding the concept of spiritual warfare (Ephesians 6:10-20)?
2. How can 2 Thessalonians 2:1-4 be harmonized with 1 John 2:18? Why are they both important for protecting the believer from discouragement and deception?
3. Try to diagram the way in which we normally think about time and the way in which the apostles viewed time. What practical difference does their way of thinking about time in relation to Christ's coming make?

Part Four

PRINCIPLES

9

THE PERILS OF "FALLING AWAY"

Now I desire to remind you, though you know all things once for all, that the Lord, after saving a people out of the land of Egypt, subsequently destroyed those who did not believe. And angels who did not keep their own domain, but abandoned their proper abode, He has kept in eternal bonds under darkness for the judgment of the great day. Just as Sodom and Gomorrah and the cities around them, since they in the same way as these indulged in gross immorality and went after strange flesh, are exhibited as an example in undergoing the punishment of eternal fire.

JUDE 5-7

Period	Persons	Peril
Old Testament	People of the Exodus	The first generation perished in the wilderness
	Fallen angels	They were consigned to hades to await judgment
	Sodom and Gomorrah	They were destroyed
New Testament	Unbelieving apostates of Jude's day	That, deceived, they will forgo the grace of God
	Harassed believers of Jude's day	That, discouraged, they will forget the grace of God

INTRODUCTION

"Why preach on judgment? You can't scare people into heaven these days!" In that way a (conservative) man of the cloth justified the fact that few contemporary preachers preach about judgment.

One simple question. And one simple assertion.

In a way our preacher friend was right. As early as twenty-five years ago a national poll revealed that whereas 73 percent of all Americans believed in life after death, fewer than 5 percent had any fear of going to hell.[1]

But he was also wrong. The truth is that preachers hesitate to preach on judgment because it is a distasteful subject, to themselves as well as to their hearers.

It was distasteful to Jude also. But he had no real choice because for him disobedience to the Spirit was more than distasteful—it was unthinkable. So his letter says more about the Christian's jeopardy than it does about the Christian's joy (v. 4). It says more about the believer's peril than it does about the believer's privileges (vv. 5-7).

Of course the very idea of a believer's standing in jeopardy of judgment runs count to the basic inclinations of all of us and to the cherished doctrines of many of us. Can it be that one can enter the faith and be saved, only to fall away from it and be lost? That is the first question many will ask upon reading Jude's warning. But is it the right question? Let us see exactly what Jude says about the perils of falling away from the faith.

"STEP RIGHT THIS WAY"

"Though you already know all this, I want to remind you," writes Jude (v. 5, NIV). There are certain episodes that one would just as soon forget. But, once again, Jude will not let us forget. So, with him, we review the facts in the following cases.

THE PEOPLE OF THE EXODUS REEXAMINED (V. 5)

There is no denying that the children of Israel had been saved out of Egypt—that ancient microcosm of the world. The chariots of Pharaoh lay rusting on the bottom of the Red Sea. Like the path

of Bunyan's pilgrim, however, Israel's path to Canaan still promised some hazardous encounters with the giant Despair and with
other giants as well. Still, if Jacob's sons entertained any doubts
whatever about Jehovah's ability to deliver His people, one look
back to that grand deliverance from Pharaoh should have been sufficient to dispel those doubts.

Nevertheless, we know that such was not the case. Israel refused
to go forward, and then God made them go back. The first generation of the Exodus perished in the wilderness. Quoting words from
the Old Testament, the writer of Hebrews sums up the divine decree
in the following fashion:

> THEREFORE I WAS ANGRY
>   WITH THIS GENERATION,
> AND SAID, "THEY ALWAYS GO
>   ASTRAY IN THEIR HEART;
> AND THEY DID NOT KNOW MY
>   WAYS";
> AS I SWORE IN MY WRATH,
> "THEY SHALL NOT ENTER MY
>   REST."
>
> HEBREWS 3:10-11

Israel was delivered from Egypt. But only those who reverently
believed God were granted entrance to the promised land. The
others perished.

Israel is exhibit number one.

THE FALLEN ANGELS RECONSIDERED (v. 6)

And what about the angels who sinned? According to Jude (and
Peter, cf. 2 Peter 2:4), a great host of them have already been consigned to hades and pits of darkness to await not a trial but final
judgment. And as for Satan himself (still going about as a roaring
lion, according to 1 Peter 5:8), his day of reckoning is coming also
(Revelation 20:10).

Unlike Israel, the devil and his angels did not begin their journey
in Egypt but in heaven. They had but to retain their favored posi-

tion—not attain or regain it. Instead, they became arrogant and rebellious.

The fallen angels become exhibit number two.

SODOM AND GOMORRAH REVISITED (v. 7)

Third, Jude points to the citizenry of Sodom and Gomorrah and nearby cities (Admah and Zeboim). Concerning the early history of those people we know little or nothing. But we do know that they were favored with a well-watered valley resembling the "garden of the Lord" and "Egypt as you go to Zoar" (Genesis 13:10). That is why Lot chose to live there.

Though there was no physical evidence of the judgments on Israel and the fallen angels, the evidence of judgment upon Sodom and Gomorrah was immediately available to Jude's readers. And it is available to us. The once verdant area became the dry, desolate, denuded region of the Dead Sea, and thus it stands out in stark contrast to the Eden it once was.

The first time we read about the people of Sodom and Gomorrah in the Scriptures, we are introduced to their sin. But it seems that they became worse and worse, and finally God called a halt to their immorality. Then judgment was inexorable and final. And, as Jude says, they "are exhibited as an example, in undergoing the punishment of eternal fire" (v. 7b).

The people of Sodom and Gomorrah constitute exhibit number three.

HOW SECURE ARE THE SAINTS?

What did the lawgiver say? "On the evidence of two or three witnesses . . ." (Deuteronomy 19:15). Jude has complied. And he has selected three witnesses carefully.

THE SIGNIFICANCE OF THE EXAMPLES

The people of Israel were en route to Canaan. They had been delivered from Egypt, but they were not "home free." Except for Caleb, Joshua, and innocent children, the generation that left Egypt never entered the promised land.

The angels, on the other hand, had known nothing but their exalted state in heaven. Far from seeking an earthly Canaan, they already enjoyed the very presence of God. They had nothing to gain by rebelling, and everything to lose. Incomprehensible though it may seem, they threw their lot in with Lucifer, who boasted, "I will ascend to heaven" (Isaiah 14:13). But instead of gaining a higher heaven, they descended to the lowest hell.

In spite of their sins, the people of Sodom and Gomorrah enjoyed the sun and the rain and the other good gifts that a loving God showers on the just and the unjust. The mercies of God coupled with the arrival of righteous Lot should have led them to repent. Instead, they progressed in immorality to the point where Lot's spirit vexed him day after day. It seems that they deliberately set out to see if a loving God could conjure up wrath. The divine answer was a rain of fire and brimstone.

Why those particular examples? Because those personages committed the primary sins of the apostates whom Jude is opposing. They did so in very different types of societies and in widely varying circumstances. And all reaped the just judgment of Jehovah God.

HOW THE EXAMPLES APPLY

But does that apply to the Church? The Body of Christ seems different from the above examples because it is composed of those who through repentance and faith have availed themselves of Christ's righteousness (2 Corinthians 5:21). It is composed of those who are "accepted in the beloved" (Ephesians 1:6, KJV). Of those who, with Paul, are convinced "that neither death, nor life, nor angels, nor principalities, nor things present, nor things to come, nor powers, nor height, nor depth, nor any other created thing, shall be able to separate us from the love of God, which is in Christ Jesus our Lord" (Romans 8:38-39).

The question, however, is not, Do Jude's examples apply to the Church? They obviously do. Rather, the question is, *How* do these examples apply to the Church? To answer the latter question, note that Jude is dealing with two classes of people in the visible Church, not one. First, there are apostate teachers, who really belong to the

world even though they are in the Church. Irrespective of their pro-
fessions of reliance on the grace of God and their pretensions to
godliness, they will meet with the same fate as did the people of the
Exodus, the fallen angels, and the citizens of Sodom and Gomorrah.

Second, there are believing saints, some of whom are in danger of
being intimidated by the presence of those sophisticated rascals or
even deceived by their proposals. The saints, therefore, should be-
ware of discouragement and deception. They should be aware of the
necessity for progressing in the faith in the assurance that God is
able to keep them from stumbling (v. 24).

But some readers will be insistent. "Tell us," they will say, "what
about the security of the believer? Can it be that the apostate teachers concerning whom Jude writes were once true believers who subsequently departed from the faith and became lost? What are the implications of Jude's warnings and admonitions?"

It would be unwise to go beyond the text of Jude's letter in an
attempt to answer such questions here. The opposing views have
been clearly delineated in literally hundreds of books. The authors
of this book themselves do not see eye to eye on all the related issues.
The important thing for Calvinists, who hold tenaciously to the doctrine of the security of the believer, is that they do not allow that
doctrine to lull them to sleep so that they cannot hear Jude's warnings. And the important thing for Arminians, who sincerely doubt
that doctrine, is that they do not become so preoccupied with Jude's
warnings that they do not take hold of his assurances.

Perhaps, however, our Western minds rush too easily to categori-
cal conclusions. True, a person is either saved or lost, a believer
or an unbeliever, born again or not born again. But although God
surely knows the spiritual state of any individual, and the individual
himself *can* know it, the exact state of any individual may be unknown to the rest of us. At any given point in time there must be
tens of thousands of people in the churches who, by virtue of con-
tact with the Word and people of God, have "escaped" from many
of the excesses and perils of the world and have attained a new understanding of the truths and blessings of the divine order. To
actually be born into the family of God they need only to make a

full commitment to Christ as Lord and Savior. The alternative is to refuse to make that commitment and remain a worldling. That refusal can take various forms. One can abandon the church and make a complete reentry into the world as either a passive unbeliever or as an active opponent of Christian truth. Or, one can re-man a worldling in the church, either as an "inactive participant" or as an active promoter of false teaching and life-style.

Before Jude lays down his pen he will have clear words for everyone in the churches. But his word to all worldings who turn their backs on the truth of God is one of judgment. Christ is Lord of *all*—the world as well as the Church.

CONCLUSION

Our age has been described as the "age of messiahs"—and rightly so. According to recent estimates, cultic leaders in America now claim a following of some two to three million adherents compared to a mere one hundred thousand just one generation ago. And the number is growing.[2] Thousands, finding little satisfaction in the empty shells of materialism and religious liberalism, have been attracted to the bizarre teachings of one or another self-proclaimed "super saint." What makes our times so unique is that this is a *worldwide* phenomenon:

> Over 6,000 of such new religious movements have been reported from Africa. Since the second world war hundreds of new religions arose in Japan and a similar number has been reported from the Philippines. The thousands of cargo cults and prophetic movements in New Guinea and Oceania are well known. . . . In Southeast Asia, from Korea to Indonesia and from Burma to South Vietnam, millions of people are finding a new meaning to life in the fellowship of such messianic movements as the Park-Chang No Kyo or the Phat Gao Hoa-Hoa.[3]

It is a sad but undeniable fact that many of those movements have their origin in apostasy from the Christian faith. Christian pastors and missionaries alike are challenged by the fact that many of those messianic leaders were at one time active in the Church. Many were trained in Christian schools and seminaries and served as church leaders, pastors, and teachers.[4]

NOTES

1. Wiel Herberg, *Protestant, Catholic and Jew* (New York: Doubleday, 1955), 72-73.
2. Peter Rowley, *New Gods in Armenia* (New York: McKay, 1971), p. 3.
3. Gottfried Oosterwal, *Modern Messianic Movements* (Elkhart: Institute of Mennonite Studies, 1973), p. 7.
4. Ibid., p. 34.

QUESTIONS FOR REFLECTION AND DISCUSSION

1. Consider the case of false teachers in the Church. In what sense have they benefited from their knowledge of God, His Word, and His people? In what sense have they "fallen away" from faith?
2. Why is it important for all true contemporary Christians to give attention to Jude's warnings and admonitions? What special significance does Jude's letter have for members of communions in which false teachers are present and even prominent?

Part Five

PREVENTATIVES

10

WORK OUT YOUR OWN SALVATION

But you, beloved, building yourselves up on your most holy faith; praying in the Holy Spirit; keep yourselves in the love of God, waiting anxiously for the mercy of our Lord Jesus Christ to eternal life. And have mercy on some, who are doubting; save others, snatching them out of the fire; and on some have mercy with fear, hating even the garment polluted by the flesh.

JUDE 20-23

The Focus	The Activity
Y O U R S E L F	1. Keep yourselves in God's love 2. Build yourselves up in your most holy faith 3. Pray in the Holy Spirit 4. Look for the mercy of God

INTRODUCTION

When speaking to a group of Christians, the educated and eloquent Hindu philosopher Sarvepalli Radhakrishnan said, "You Christians seem to be a group of ordinary people making some extraordinary claims." His hearers responded, "We make no claims

115

for ourselves but only for Jesus Christ our Lord." But Radhakrishnan was not a man to be so easily silenced. He replied, "All right. But why should I expect him to do more for me than he seems to have done for you?"[1]

It is not enough to oppose heretical teaching and behavior. One must also exemplify holy teaching and behavior. Jude has provided us with a portrait of the false teacher. Now he provides us with a portrait of the true disciple—not in detail but in bold outline.

"But you, beloved . . ." (v. 20). Using that tender term for the third time, Jude turns his attention to true Christians. His words are reminiscent of those employed by the author of Hebrews who, after forthrightly describing the state of apostates, says, "But, beloved, we are convinced of better things concerning you, and things that accompany salvation, though we are speaking in this way" (Hebrews 6:9).

Possessing the same confidence, Jude uses a series of verbs that constitute a course of Christian behavior in the face of error—preventatives of apostasy. Sighing and crying, hand-wringing, and even soul-searching are not sufficient. Embattled believers must take more positive steps toward working out their own salvation (vv. 20-21) and working for the salvation of others (vv. 22-23).

Paul's exhortation to the Philippians—"Work out your salvation" (Philippians 2:12)—is certainly an appropriate way to sum up Jude's first four preventatives. The surest way to ward off disease is to give attention to the rules of healthful living. Moreover, those who would aid the weak should keep themselves strong.

"KEEP YOURSELVES IN THE LOVE OF GOD" (v. 21)

Grammatically, "keep" is the most important verb in verses 20 and 21. The other verbs are participles and tell what is involved in keeping oneself in God's love.

Henry Alford says that the construction means that we should keep ourselves *in the sphere of* God's love.[2] But "God so loved *the world* that He gave His only begotten Son" (John 3:16, italics added). How then can we draw circles and say, "This is the sphere of God's love," or, "This is outside the sphere of God's love"?

If God's love is unbounded, how can we take Jude seriously when he says, "Keep yourselves in the love of God"? Well, our only recourse is to look in the Scripture and see if and where the boundaries should be drawn.

The Greek word for world in John 3:16 is *kosmos*. It has several meanings in the New Testament. First, it means "the ordered world," that which we would call the created universe (John 1:10). Second, it means the world of mankind and is almost synonymous with *oikoumenē gē,* the "inhabited earth." It is the world of men and women, which God loved and for which He gave His Son (John 3:16). Third, it means "the disordered world," the "this world" that is in the vice-grip of Satan (1 John 5:19). In this third sense it means much the same as *aiōn* (the "present age"), a word that is also translated "world." It is "this world" that had gotten into the churches in the persons of false teachers.

Universalism confuses those worlds. It says that God loves all three and will reconcile all three to Himself. The Scriptures, on the other hand, teach that the created world was good but was "invaded" and partly "occupied" by Satan. He has thereby established "his world" within God's good created world. The inhabited world of mankind has become a battleground in this "war of the worlds."

It is John—the one so close to his Lord—who speaks most about the "disordered *kosmos*" and who writes concerning it: "Do not love the world, nor the things in the world. If anyone loves the world, the love of the Father is not in him. For all that is in the world, the lust of the flesh and the lust of the eyes and the boastful pride of life, is not from the Father, but is from the world. And the world is passing away, and also its lusts; but the one who does the will of God abides forever" (1 John 2:15-17).

John also warns us: "Watch yourselves, that you might not lose what we have accomplished, but that you may receive a full reward. Anyone who goes too far and does not abide in the teaching of Christ, does not have God; the one who abides in the teaching, he has both the Father, and the Son" (2 John 8-9).

All of that reinforces Jude's previous warnings and his present admonition. Jude has not been talking about our "stumblings"—

he will deal with them in verse 24. He has been talking about "falling away" from the truth; about "facing in" toward God, and then turning around and "heading out" into the world; about knowing where the boundary is and deliberately moving in the wrong direction and crossing over it.

There is a "bent," or "direction," to every life. There is a passion that will master all other passions. "We love Him," writes John, "because He first loved us" (1 John 4:19, KJV). Then *"keep"* yourselves in God's love," says Jude. In this admonition he echoes our Lord who said, "I [have] loved you. Abide in my love" (John 15:9, RSV).* Jude then proceeds to give directions as to how one can remain in that privileged place.

"BUILDING YOURSELVES UP ON YOUR MOST HOLY FAITH"

Jude's exhortation reminds us of verse 3: "Contend . . . for the faith which was once for all delivered to the saints." The "faith" is objective in both cases. It is the "most holy faith," the true teaching, the divine doctrine of God's holy Word. As for the believer's subjective faith in God, that cannot be strengthened merely by willing it to be so. It is strengthened as a part of the process of building up oneself in apostolic teaching (Romans 10:13). In short, we are to study the Bible and build our lives upon its truths.

There are three primary groupings of church people with respect to the study of the Scriptures. First, there are those who do not consider the Bible to be absolutely unique and authoritative, to be "most holy." They may *read* it as part of their liturgy. They may *refer* to it in their sermons and on solemn occasions; but they do not *rely* upon it as a "sure word of prophecy." Second, there are those who believe the Bible to be what it claims to be—the very Word of God. They are ready to *expose* the error of teachers who detract from its authority; they insist that it be *expounded* in their pulpits and classrooms; but they do not personally *explore* its content in accordance with the divine injunction (2 Timothy 2:15). Third, there are those who not only *subscribe* to the Bible and *sit* at the feet of preachers and teachers who minister its truth, but who also

*Revised Standard Version.

search the Scriptures for themselves in order to properly evaluate what they hear (Acts 17:11) and in order to grow as God's children (1 Peter 2:2).

Those in the first group should avail themselves of some book that deals forthrightly with the problem of the trustworthiness of the Bible. Most lay people will find books like *Our Infallible Bible* and *Focus on Fact: Why You Can Trust the Bible* most helpful.[3] They should also actually study the Scriptures, either alone (with helpful published tools for Bible study) or with a group of people who believe the Bible and are not riding some doctrinal hobbyhorse.

Those in the second group should consider their vulnerability. As long as they employ reliable preachers and teachers, and as long as they enjoy the privileges of freedom, they may make some progress in the building process. But let some persuasive Bible teacher take a detour from sound doctrine, and many of them will blindly follow. Or let them be placed in a situation where they must rely upon God's Word alone, and they may fall apart spiritually.

Many Christians will remember *The Hiding Place*—the film or the book. They will recall the terrible risks that were taken by Betsy and Corrie ten Boom in order to keep their precious Bible. Think of the light that the sacred Book brought to the barbarous existence of Barracks 28 at Ravensbruck:

> Sometimes I would slip the Bible from its little sack with hands that shook, so mysterious had it become to me. It was new; it had just been written. I marveled sometimes that the ink was dry. I had believed the Bible always, but reading it now had nothing to do with belief. It was simply a description of the way things were—of hell and heaven, of how men act and how God acts. I had read a thousand times the story of Jesus' arrest—how soldiers had slapped Him, laughed at Him, flogged Him. Now such happenings had faces and voices.[4]

Enter the third group. Study the Word, dear Christian. *Build yourselves* up in the faith. So much has been given. Something is also required. Settle on a system. Then take the time to master some part of the Bible each day. And live by it, knowing that man does not—cannot—"LIVE ON BREAD ALONE, BUT ON EVERY WORD THAT PROCEEDS OUT OF THE MOUTH OF GOD" (Matthew 4:4).

"PRAYING IN THE HOLY SPIRIT" (v. 20)

One does not contend for the faith simply by argumentation—by giving a reason for the hope that is within him (1 Peter 3:15). One does not counteract heresy and worldliness whether in the church or in his own life by study alone. "Prayer is the Christian's native breath, the Christian's vital air," says the songwriter.

The word "prayer" is *proseuchē*. Praying involves "facing toward" (*pros*) and prayer or worship (*euchē*). "In [*en*] the Spirit" indicates the source of power for prayer. So, with characteristic economy of words, Jude gives us the "posture," predisposition, and power of true prayer. Briefly examine them.

First, true prayer may be offered in any posture: sitting, standing, kneeling, or lying down. It makes no difference as far as God is concerned, though it may make a difference as far as the concentration and attitude of the one who prays is concerned. But it is essential that the Christian "face God"—not physically like the Muslim who faces Mecca because he believes God is in heaven and cannot be located by the point of the compass. But, as we saw in the previous section, the Christian must be "facing in" toward God, not "heading out" toward the world.

Second, true prayer involves the predisposition to worship. The two go together. Jesus said, "Pray, then, in this way: 'Our Father who art in heaven, hallowed be Thy name' " (Matthew 6:9). It is that hallowing of the name that reveals the attitude with which one should come to the place of prayer.

Third, true prayer finds its source of *power* in the Holy Spirit. The object of prayer is not so much getting *our* will done as it is getting *His* will done on earth as well as in heaven (Matthew 6:10). If we ask according to His will He hears us and we receive what we ask of Him (1 John 5:14). The true end of prayer is to realize His will. That is why it is essential that we pray "in the Spirit." As Paul explains, "In the same way the Spirit also helps our weakness; for we do not know how to pray as we should, but the Spirit Himself intercedes for us with groanings too deep for words; and He who searches the hearts knows what the mind of the Spirit is, because He intercedes for the saints according to the will of God" (Romans 8:26-27).

The "learned" teachers Jude speaks of have given up on prayer. Or, if they pray, they pray to be seen of men as was the case with the hypocrites to whom our Lord referred in Matthew 6:5.

One of the most hopeful signs in some of our churches today is that their members still pray, corporately and privately. One cannot visit the early morning prayer meetings in Korea, for example, without carrying away the conviction that when the final report on the great growth of many Korean churches is given it will reveal the influence of those early morning prayer meetings for which Korean Christians are well known.

By the same token, one of the most disheartening aspects of church life in the West is a decline in the time and attention given to prayer. In church after church, the attendance at the prayer service is barely 5 to 10 percent of the attendance at the Sunday morning worship service. Admittedly, 11:00 A.M. on Sunday morning is as appropriate for prayer as is 5:00 A.M. or 7:30 P.M. on a weekday—perhaps more so. But what would happen to Sunday morning attendance if the hallowed hour (or hour and a quarter—no more) were to be stripped of announcements, choir anthems, and liturgical embellishments, and the accumulated time were given to prayers by the people Again, admittedly, church members who do not gather for corporate prayer in the church can pray privately in home or office. But do they? And, in any case, does the latter take the place of the former?

"WAITING . . . FOR THE MERCY" (V. 21)

"Wait" may be too weak a word to express what Jude has in mind. *Prosdechomai* means to "wait with expectation." Jude says that even believers need the mercy of God as exhibited in the giving of His life on the cross and in the granting of eternal life in the future.

It is precisely here that false teachers often become most convincing. Having downgraded the significance of Christ's cross, they now denigrate the solace of His coming. Having embraced the world that now is, they eschew the world that is to come.

True Christians are hard pressed to keep a proper balance between working and waiting, between their efforts on behalf of this life and their expectations for a better life to come. The whole inhabited world cries out for justice, for nourishment, for concern. Meanwhile, the whole evil-permeated world of which Satan is god persists in its denial of the only rule that can right its recurring wrongs.

What is to be done? Scripture demands that believers care for the poor, especially those of the household of faith (Galatians 6:10). But there is nothing in Scripture that leads us to think that the mercy of Christians will radically change "this world" into anything approaching an earthly utopia. If that is our expectation we are doomed to disappointment and disillusionment. Christian believers themselves—not just some of them but all of them—wait for the mercy of the Lord Jesus Christ to bring them to eternal life.

Conclusion

Faith, hope, and love—Jude emphasizes all three, as do the other apostles. But he applies each in his own way and according to the requirements of Christians whose churches have been infiltrated by fifth columnists with other loyalties, fifth columnists who challenge the purity of the church and the faith of believers.

In times like these, Christians can rest in the finished work of Christ. They can rejoice in their salvation. That is a part of their "most holy faith."

> There was no other good enough
> To pay the price of sin;
> He only could unlock the gate
> Of heav'n and let us in.
>
> Cecil F. Alexander

But they can do more. They can *build* on that faith. They can *keep* themselves in the love of Christ. They can *pray* in the Spirit. They can *live* in hope of eternal life. In a word, they can *work out* their salvation.

Certainly one must come to rest in the finished work of Christ. Without that there is no salvation at all. But the believer must keep coming to Christ for strength to move forward. It is absolutely certain that one cannot "fall away" while he is "moving forward." Perhaps the late Ethel Waters said it in a way that will register for most of us. Unencumbered by the theological sophistication that has a way of making mouths dumb and paralyzing pens, she wrote, "We've got to keep on—keep, *keep!* Don't let up. I know I haven't learned it yet, but I'm crawlin'! I'm crawlin'! You can get in a rut with Jesus when what He wants is to keep you coming to Him constantly, to teach you something new, something fresh. He wants to keep you *clinging* to Him. Because once you think you're *stapled* to Him, you're no good."[5]

Ethel Waters might have been "crawlin'," but she was moving in the right direction. And she ended up crawlin' right through the gates of heaven!

NOTES

1. Arne Sovik, *Salvation Today* (Minneapolis: Augsburg House, 1973), p. 28.
2. Henry Alford, *The Greek Testament,* 4 vols. (Chicago: Moody, 1958), 4:541.
3. David Nettleton, *Our Infallible Bible* (Schaumberg, Ill.: Regular Baptist, 1977); John F. MacArthur, Jr., *Focus on Fact: Why You Can Trust the Bible* (Old Tappan, N.J.: Revell, 1977).
4. Corrie ten Boom with John and Elizabeth Sherrill, *The Hiding Place* (Washington Depot, Conn.: Chosen Books, 1971), p. 28.
5. Ethel Waters, *To Me It's Wonderful* (New York: Harper & Row, 1972), p. 50.

QUESTIONS FOR REFLECTION AND DISCUSSION

1. Why is it important to distinguish between the "worlds" mentioned in the various English translations of the New Testament?
2. What is the relationship between building oneself up in the holy faith and exercising faith in God and His Word?
3. How would you evaluate the strength of the prayer life exhibited by Christians and churches with which you are familiar? What about your prayer life?
4. In what ways are working and waiting for the Lord compatible?

11

WORK FOR THE SALVATION OF OTHERS

And have mercy on some, who are doubting; save others, snatching them out of the fire; and on some have mercy with fear, hating even the garment polluted by the flesh.

JUDE 22-23

Focus	The Activity
O T H E R S	1. Convince the doubters 2. Save the unwary 3. Care for the "contaminated"

INTRODUCTION

It may seem that Jude has confused his priorities. In the face of an invasion of the Church by the world he issues apostolic instructions to look after the first person singular. In effect he is saying, "Work out your own salvation." Only then does he direct us to work for the salvation of others.

Odd? Not at all. A moment of reflection will convince us that he is right. Were the concern for creature comforts or consolation, the Christian order would be others first and oneself second. When it comes to salvation from the world, however, only the saved one can save another. One is in no position to save a companion who is struggling to free himself from quicksand unless he himself stands on solid ground.

When you and I build on the faith, pray in the Spirit, keep in God's love, and look for Christ's mercy, then we are in a position to help others. But we must not try to help them in a blind, unthinking way. Why? Because, there are at least three classes of people who require help—especially in times of apostasy. And they have somewhat different needs.

First, some are plagued by doubts. Second, some stand on the brink of judgment without so much as a qualm. Third, some get caught up in the fleshly living that often accompanies false thinking. We must respond somewhat differently to those people. At least, Jude's words in verses 22 and 23 seem to suggest this.

Convince the Doubter

The Bishop of Woolwich (John A. T. Robinson) to whom we referred earlier writes that we are on the brink of a period when a defense of Christian truth will be required. He allows for the fact that some Christians "see the best, and indeed the only, defense of doctrine to lie in the firm reiteration, in fresh and contemporary language, of 'the faith once delivered to the saints.' "[1] He believes, however, that "if our defense of the Faith is limited to this, we shall find in all likelihood that we have lost out to all but a tiny religious remnant."[2] That is why he advocates a "radical recasting" in which "the most fundamental categories of our theology—of God, of supernatural, and of religion itself—must go into the melting."[3]

It would be difficult to find a statement that more clearly highlights our task vis-à-vis doubters—doubters in the world and doubters in the Church. When Robinson says a defense of the faith is required, he is right. When he advocates a "radical recasting," he is wrong. Why? What should we do for doubters?

First, we begin by acknowledging the sincerity of many doubters. In and of itself, doubt is a temptation, not necessarily a sin. Probably every thinking Christian has entertained doubt at one time or another. Why? Not because the "faith once for all delivered to the saints" is imperfect, but because the saints to whom the faith has been entrusted are imperfect. The world is too much with us. And the world through its wisdom does not know God (1 Corinthians 1:21).

Doubt, therefore, is understandable. But it is also dangerous, because God does not excuse it. The doubter needs help. But he needs help of the right kind.

Second, notice what Jude says we should do in order to help the doubter. His instruction consists of but one word, and, because of a manuscript problem, we cannot be sure whether that word is "show mercy" or "convince/convict" (those words have similar beginnings and endings in Greek). Translations, therefore, differ. Alford opts for "convince/convict."[4] We agree.

Our former friend and colleague Paul Little left contemporary Christians a notable legacy in the form of a small book entitled *Know Why You Believe.*[5] It is important to know *what* we believe—to know the faith once for all entrusted to the saints. But, it is also important to know *why* we believe—to be "ready to make a defense to everyone who asks you to give an account for the hope that is in you" (1 Peter 3:15). Our faith does not rest on reason, but our faith is reasonable. The doubter needs to be convinced of that. Since doubts usually have an intellectual dimension, their resolution usually has an intellectual dimension as well. We need not be afraid of that fact.

If Alford is correct, Jude's word is *elenchein,* and that is the same word used by our Lord when He promised that the Holy Spirit would come to convince (or convict) the world of guilt in regard to sin, righteousness, and judgment (John 16:8). (Note that carefully, because Jude had learned from Jesus). We have a "convincing Ally" in the Holy Spirit. There is much that we can do to help the doubter. For example, we can show him that the world's philosophies cancel each other out. Or, we can show him that the manuscript evidence for the Scriptures is far more convincing than that of Plato's *Dialogues* and many classics he accepts as genuine without question. But when one comes to the "bottom line," it is impossible by human reason to convince someone that not believing in Jesus is sin, that there is a perfect standard of righteousness even though the Perfect One is no longer on earth where we can see and hear Him firsthand, and that the "prince of this world" (Satan) has been judged at the cross of Christ. Who can convince the doubter of such truths? The Holy Spirit! He is the "Convincer."

We do our small part. We help the doubter—patiently, lovingly, mercifully, intelligently trying to demonstrate that Jesus indeed is both Lord and Christ, that the "faith once for all delivered to the saints" is truly trustworthy. We do that with a full realization of our limitations and the limitations of all human understanding. But we do it with full confidence that the Holy Spirit, the Paraclete, has been sent by our risen Christ to stand beside us and speak through us and especially through the Scriptures themselves, in a way that can cause a doubting Thomas to exclaim, "My Lord and my God" (John 20:28).

Jude says, "Convince the doubters."

SAVE THE UNWARY

There is another class of people that needs special help. They are in danger of burning. They stand on the precipice of hell. There is an urgency about their plight. Jude's pen writes in bold letters: "Save them."

There are many questions we would like to ask the apostle: Who are these people? What have they done—or what have they not done—to come into such a perilous place? Why do they not recognize the danger? How can it be that as mere mortals we are responsible to save them? How should we go about it? But Jude is not deterred by such questions. In fact, he is arrestingly brief. It is as though he were crying, "Fire! Snatch—save!"

To be sure, the "faith once for all delivered to the saints" includes enough profundities to last the most gifted among us a lifetime and beyond. But those profundities are not elevators designed to transport us into ivory towers far removed from elementary truths of God's Word and the fundamental tragedies of human existence. The faith speaks first of all to man's basic need for salvation.

There are some simple tests to apply to any theology of the human condition. First, what does it say about hell? We have some twentieth-century teachers who say that biblical pictures of hell simply constitute a means of motivating men to do what is right. Others say that the language is figurative and therefore should not be allowed to offend our human sensibilities. Others say that the only hell that exists is to be discovered in the injustices, inhumanities, and slaveries of earth. Still others deny any hell whatsoever. But the loving Christ, the beloved John, the determined Jude—these and other first-century teachers spoke of hell as a place of flaming fire to which unbelievers would certainly be consigned (Matthew 10:28; Revelation 21:8).

Second, what does the theology in question say about man's lostness? Some modern teachers say that man's "lostness" is real but not radical. Man is innately good and can save himself. Others say say that his "lostness" is temporary—that if in this life he is not saved, he will be given a second chance in the life to come. Still others deny that man is "lost" at all. But the all-knowing Christ, the learned Paul, the inspired Jude—these and other first-century leaders made clear that man is hopelessly lost unless divine help is forthcoming (Luke 19:10; Romans 3:10, 23; Ephesians 2:8-9).

Third, what does the theology in question say about the Christian's responsibility? Some contemporary theologians say that our responsibility is to live exemplary lives and to teach others to be kind, loving, and good. Others say that we are to take whatever social and political action is necessary to change society so that man can be fully "human" and free. Few, if any, would deny that we have some responsibility. But the suffering Jesus, the chastened Peter, the distressed Jude—these and other first-century pathfinders of the faith insisted that we must do all that we can to save men from the just judgment of God (John 5:28-29; Acts 2:38-41).

Any theology or teaching that obscures either the unbeliever's lostness or the believer's responsibility to save him, is unchristian. As a matter of fact, the people Jude has in mind seem to be people who are quite innocent, quite unknowing. Nevertheless, they are in danger of fire even though they may not really be aware of it. Jude says, "Try to save them." Had he used the word *susate* it would mean that we have the power to save them. Jude used another construction—*sōzete*—which is best translated "attempt to save" them.[6] And do it with a sense of urgency—try to snatch them from the fire.

CARE FOR THE "CONTAMINATED"

Finally, there is a third class of people. It may not be entirely exclusive of those in the other two classes. But in Jude's mind its members are characterized by one distinctive—they are "contaminated." They need help, they need saving, but they represent a very real danger. Why? Because they might infect the helping, witnessing believer. So Jude says, "On some have mercy with fear, hating even the garment polluted by the flesh" (v. 23b).

Unsaved persons of that type are all around us: the worldling who wants the believer to attend his party before he will attend the believer's church; the drinker who insists that we imbibe if we want to talk; the despondent woman who reaches out to the male counselor.

How many Christian pastors and workers have had their testimonies ruined because they did not possess a healthy mixture of mercy and fear in handling such cases? Only God knows all of them. But almost all of us know some of them. If only they had studied Jude's letter. What could be more concise yet clear, more succinct yet definitive? There are people who desperately need saving. We are to show mercy toward them. But they have the potential for poisoning our lives and destroying our testimonies. That potential is to be feared.

If we have not attained the kind of holiness that hates even the clothing that is contaminated, we have not attained the mixture of mercy and fear that is required. The nonswimmer should throw a rope to the drowning man, but he should not jump into the water with him lest both drown together.

CONCLUSION

So much is wrong with the world. And so much of the world has gotten into the Church. The struggle seems to be unending.

The temptation is to say, "What's the use," and concentrate on "Number One," oneself. Jude says that attitude is only half right. It is true that we must "work out our own salvation." But for the true believer there is more to do, both in the world and in the Church. Ascertain the kind of worldlings who constitute our responsibility. Then work for their salvation—convincingly, urgently, mercifully, fearfully. And do it in dependence upon the Holy Spirit who faithfully leads men to the Christ who really saves.

NOTES

1. John A. T. Robinson, *Honest to God* (Philadelphia: Westminster, 1963), p. 7.
2. Ibid.
3. Ibid.
4. Henry Alford, *The Greek Testament*, 4 vols. (Chicago: Moody, 1958), 4:541-42.
5. Paul E. Little, *Know Why You Believe* (Wheaton, Ill.: Scripture Press, 1967).
6. Alford, 8:542.

QUESTIONS FOR REFLECTION AND DISCUSSION

1. Why is it patently impossible to defend the faith by "recasting" it? Does the faith need defending? If so, in what ways can it be defended?
2. Ask some dedicated Christians whom you know whether or not they ever entertained doubts concerning their faith, what doubts they entertained, and what they did about their doubts. What do you learn from their experience?
3. To what extent do we as contemporary Christians share Jude's conviction concerning the lostness of men? Is that conviction important? Why?
4. What do you think about the assertion that we have to join unbelievers in their worldly pursuits if we are to win them to Christ and His Church? Is it valid or invalid?

Part Six

PRAISE

12

THE ASCRIPTION OF PRAISE

Now to Him who is able to keep you from stumbling, and to make you stand in the presence of His glory blameless with great joy, to the only God our Savior, through Jesus Christ our Lord, be glory, majesty, dominion and authority, before all time and now and forever. Amen.

JUDE 24-25.

The Person of God	The omnipotent God—"Now to Him who is able"
	The only true God—"the only God our Savior"
	The eternal God—"before all time and now and forever"
The implied promise	Protection from falling Perfection in His presence
The ascription of praise	Glory Majesty Power Authority

INTRODUCTION

How often have Christians heard Jude's benediction: "Now to him who is able . . ."? What unsurpassed sublimity! What resplendent certitude! It presents the One who is from everlasting to everlasting. It promises protection in this world and perfection in the next. It prescribes praise to the One who alone is worthy of praise.

Such a doxology must be appropriate at the close of any gathering of believers. And assuredly it is. But it is especially appropriate after a study of Jude's epistle.

We lose something, you see, when we dip into the Word of God more or less willy-nilly and extract whatever seems to be to our liking.

Think for a moment. What would be the ratio of the number of times you have heard Jude's *benediction* (vv. 24-25) as compared to the number of times you have heard Jude's *admonition* (vv. 3-23)? Ten to one? One hundred to one? Perhaps one thousand to one would not be too far-fetched for some of us. As a matter of fact, the number of regular attenders in our churches who have *never* heard their preachers and teachers emphasize Jude's words of warning and exhortation must be legion. Yet those preachers and teachers use Jude's benediction regularly.

What a sad state of affairs. It is in the face of heresy and apostasy in the Church that Jude turns to God. It is in the face of a prophecy of judgment that Jude prescribes praise. It is after exhortations to work and witness that Jude promises protection.

Do we see the connection? Jude's benediction is an expression of faith that the saints will be delivered when the "faith once delivered" is under siege. The warning and the benediction should be kept together. It is by virtue of the "faith once delivered to the saints" that we know that the saints will be delivered. Where there is true doctrine and faithful discipline there can be resounding doxology—even when the days are dark. Without the faith that is factual and objective, the faith that is feeling and subjective may evaporate. Without scriptural discipline, songs in the night may give way to whistling in the dark.

The God of Heaven—His Person

Our Lord instructed His disciples, "And when these things begin to come to pass, then look up, and lift up your heads; for your redemption draweth nigh" (Luke 21:28, KJV). Jude has been looking around in the world and in the Church. Now in his final words he looks up to the God of heaven: "To him who is able . . . to the only God our Savior, through Jesus Christ our Lord. . . . Amen."

In times like these it is imperative that we see God as He truly is. Many liberal theologians have been saying that modern man can no longer believe in a God "way up there in heaven somewhere." So they attempt to "pull Him down to earth" and remake Him into a form more to the liking of modern man. True Christians, of course, will have none of that. Our Lord said, "Pray, then, in this way: 'Our Father . . . in heaven . . .'" (Matthew 6:9). God is everywhere, but His special abode is heaven. And that is where we want Him to be because that is where we are going.

But even true Christians are prone to lose sight of *who* God really is even though they know *where* He is! And in times like those described by Jude, it is absolutely essential that no one be justified in pointing an accusing finger and saying, "Your God is too small." We need a "big" God. And Jude's closing words remind us that we have a "big" God.

THE OMNIPOTENT GOD—"NOW TO HIM WHO IS ABLE"

God is all-powerful. He really is. The believer may still have some unanswered questions after studying Jude's letter. But the study made and the conditions surveyed, he is assured that God is able. Able to work all things after the counsel of His own will. Able to care for all His children.

> He is able to deliver thee,
> He is able to deliver thee;
> Tho' by sin oppressed, go to Him for rest;
> "Our God is able to deliver thee."
>
> WILLIAM A. OGDEN

The gods of the heathen often fight among themselves and neutralize each other. Never forget, dear Christian, your God is all-powerful. He is able to deliver you.

THE ONE TRUE GOD—"THE ONLY GOD OUR SAVIOR"

Some manuscripts include the word "wise," and since the King James Version includes it, that is the way most church people will remember Jude's benediction. Of course, He is omniscient. He is the "only wise God." So if that turns out to be the correct text we can gratefully accept it. But some of the best manuscripts have "to the only God." That is fundamental. Of course, He is the only wise God, the only powerful God. Why? Because he is all-wise and all-powerful? Yes. But, even more basically, *because He is the only God.* There is none other.

The unsophisticated pagans of the non-Christian world may have their *metal* (and wooden and stone) gods. In Hinduism the Absolute is the impersonal Brahma. Personal gods are numerous, but none is absolute. The sophisticated pagans of the "Christian world" may have their mental and materialistic gods. They change with current fashions. None has final validity. "All the gods of the peoples are idols," says the psalmist (Psalm 96:5). There is but one true God, Jude reminds us. And He is our Savior.

THE ETERNAL GOD—"BEFORE ALL TIME AND NOW AND FOREVER"

If praise is ascribed to this one Person before all time, in the present, and forever, it can mean but one thing: He is the *eternal* God. In the beginning He was. In the present He is. In the future He will be. "From everlasting to everlasting, Thou are God," writes the psalmist (Psalm 90:1).

The "suffering" that Buddha said is characteristic of our human condition is the realization of the transitoriness of all things. But Buddha was only partially correct. Heaven and earth may ever change and even pass away. But God will not pass away. He changes never. Jude's benediction is not intended as a theological statement as such. But it rests upon sound theology—upon the nature of God Himself—as does the hope of the Church and every Christian.

THE IMPLIED PROMISE

The fact that God is who He is provides assurance for the believer. Assurance of what? Assurance of precisely that which the believer needs most when the world invades the Church and threatens to engulf the saints: protection on earth and perfection in heaven.

PROTECTION FROM FALLING

He is able to *keep* us. The Greek word is different from that translated "keep" in verses 1 and 21. There the word is *tēreō*—"to keep an eye on," "to carefully watch over someone or something." Here in verse 24 it is *phulassō*—"to watch by night, to guard, to preserve."

And "falling" is not "falling away" as in apostasy. Of course He is able to keep us from that. It is "stumbling"—He is able to keep us from stumbling as we travel along the pathway of faith.

PERFECTION IN HIS PRESENCE

And what about the world to come? There we will be without fault or blemish. The word is the same one used by Peter in his reference to Christ as the sacrificial Lamb of God (1 Peter 1:18-19). Imagine walking through this evil world as members of churches assailed by worldlings and ending up perfected and in God's presence!

More, we will be in His presence with great joy. But then, the psalmist had said it long before: "Thou wilt make known to me the path of life; in Thy presence is fulness of joy; in Thy right hand there are pleasures forever" (Psalm 16:11).

Impossible? With man, yes. But not with God. That is the point. Believe it. He is able to protect and perfect. Jude's benediction is not primarily intended as a promise to Christians. But the promise is there. And it should support the Church and gladden the heart of every Christian.

THE ASCRIPTION OF PRAISE

So to God our Savior be glory, majesty, dominion, and authority.

Glory—the *doxa* of doxology. Basically glory refers to the honor resulting from a good opinion or estimate.

Majesty—from *megas,* or great. Essentially, God's majesty refers to His greatness and dignity.

Dominion—is *kratos.* It can also be translated as "power" or "strength."

Authority—is *exousia,* from a verb meaning "it is lawful." It refers to the freedom and ability to do as one chooses, the right to rule with the expectation that others will obey.

Upon reflection it will be seen that those are attributes of God now being ascribed to God through the Mediator—our Lord Christ. Jude is openly acknowledging God to be who He already is. Praise does not add something to God. It does not make Him something that He has not already been in the past or something that He would not otherwise be in the future. Rather, praise acknowledges God to be the Person He already is and always will be. And that is incredibly important because when, in the world to come, God is God to all His creatures, *all will be well with that world.* One might say that though praise does not change God into someone He otherwise would not be or add something to God that He does not already possess, it does change *us* and it does add something to *us.* It helps change us into something we were reborn to be—Christlike persons. And it adds a dimension of life we were reborn to exhibit—triumph. The gates of hell will not prevail. Beleaguered and besieged, the Church militant will become the Church triumphant—through Jesus Christ our Lord. Amen.

QUESTIONS FOR REFLECTION AND DISCUSSION

1. Why is Jude's concluding benediction made all the more significant by the context in which it occurs?
2. Think of as many objective results of praise to God as you can.
3. What are some subjective results of praise?

Moody Press, a ministry of the Moody Bible Institute, is designed for education, evangelization, and edification. If we may assist you in knowing more about Christ and the Christian life, please write us without obligation: Moody Press, c/o MLM, Chicago, Illinois 60610.